Traveling Light

Free Yourself from the Crap in your Head

Angela Belford

Traveling Light by Angela Belford
Published by CBC Global
PO Box 1851, Fayetteville, AR 72702

www.AngelaBelford.com

info@AngelaBelford.com

Book Design, Layout and Cover by Elizabeth Kirkendall and Hilary Saunders at The Belford Group.

ISBN: 978-0-9991862-2-0

For information about special discounts available for bulk purchases, sales promotions, fund-raising and educational needs, contact CBC Global/The Belford Group at 479-443-9945 or sales@AngelaBelford.com

.

Contents

Chapter 1
Let's get this trip started

How it all began

I stood in my room, water dripping from the pajama pants and scarf of the salwar kameez I bought when I landed in Chennai 11 days earlier. After days of scorching heat, air pollution, and constant noise from honking cars, the rain suddenly came over the city, cooling it and muffling the noise. Dancing seemed like the most logical and appropriate response. We danced and felt the water run down our faces, saw how the rain looked in the street lamps, smelled fresh air for the first time in days, and listened to most of my team and the Indian friends we'd made laughing at our silliness. We danced and laughed and felt free.

I was in Chennai as part of a trip with my church. We had gone there to explore opportunities to support a school and do some construction projects. Naturally, I wanted to be completely prepared for the experience. During the six months of planning for the trip, I attended cultural training and researched as best I could in the early days of the World Wide Web to find out where to shop, where to find food, and where to exchange money without Google Maps or a travel website. In the name of preparation, I packed a backpack, a rolling bag, and a HUGE suitcase with a warehouse-club-size jar of peanut butter, crackers, electric converters, different outfits for every day, flip flops, tennis shoes, dress shoes, sandals, extra underwear, jewelry, chargers, snacks, bathing suit, notebook, journal, Bible, pens, small purse, passport lanyard holder, belts, scarves, hats, and Lord knows what else. I grew my hair longer to use fewer products and hair appliances. I also packed a small rolling bag with several outfits in case my luggage got lost, additional shoes, a regular camera, a video camera, books – nonfiction and fiction depending on my mood, more snacks, and travel games. Whatever was gonna happen, I was ready for it.

After about a week there, I met Mike Compton, who ran an organization supporting aid workers. He traveled the world with two shirts, two pairs of pants that zip off to shorts, three pairs of boxers, and a white tank top undershirt in a backpack with deodorant, a toothbrush, a Bible, and a journal. He told me he went to a laundromat once a week and wore the undershirt and boxers while he washed the rest of the clothes. And it planted a seed in my mind...what if (just maybe) I could live with that kind of freedom, too?

As the rain stopped and our dancing slowed, I felt elated. For once, I wasn't hot and sticky. I thought about the huge suitcase in the corner of my dorm room and wondered why I had brought it. Tomorrow, I would begin the trek back to my real life and would have to lug that suitcase through the Chennai airport to Gatwick in London, where I'd have to take a taxi instead of the Tube with my team because I couldn't manage the huge bag, my rolling bag, and a backpack. I'd then have to lug all that baggage over to Heathrow airport to check it and then pick it up in baggage claim three days from now when my family picked me up from the airport. What had I even put in that bag that seemed so important? I went back to my room, sat down on the bed, and opened the giant suitcase I'd barely touched in the last week. The crackers were smooshed and uneaten. The bathing suit still rolled in its corner. Oh good, I still had the 64 oz. can of peanut butter, unopened. That had clearly come in handy.

It would take many years before I came to understand that most of the items in the large suitcase were only there to mitigate my fear. I didn't need them. Turns out I'd been doing the same thing in my life -- collecting things I didn't need to assuage fears that weren't connected to the realities of my life anymore.

Maybe you can relate?

Because while you might not have laid in bed at age five wondering why mom and dad didn't care enough about you to keep even a jar of peanut butter in the house so you wouldn't go to bed hungry, you have your own traumas and bad memories, and the coping skills you developed as a child as workarounds. Some of them have likely served you very well. And maybe it's time to let some of them go so you can do other things. That's what this book is about.

Twenty years later, I can travel with two pairs of black stretchy pants that pass for yoga pants and dress pants, three shirts, and a jacket. Could I bring more? Sure. Do I sometimes choose to bring more? Absolutely. But the freedom of knowing I can get those $24 "no checked bags" plane tickets to fly to Orlando has been literally life-changing.

Are you ready to put down some of that old baggage too? The rubbish of broken relationships, broken promises, abandonment, fear of failure, fear of success, or trauma all add up over time. The good news is, you can put it down. The bad news is the unpacking process might be kinda gross. And that's why we're doing this together because, believe me when I tell you, nobody goes through this process alone.

Just consider me the Obi-Wan to your Luke.

The hero's journey: what you, me, and Luke Skywalker have in common.

I'm kind of obsessed with Joseph Campbell's concept of the hero's journey, and I'm in good company. In fact, after reading Campbell, George Lucas wrote the original Star Wars movie, which is quite possibly the most beautiful example of this concept.

Campbell's thesis is that there are a series of similar plot lines that come up over and over again throughout human mythology and history. No matter where you are in the world (or universe!), you'll see the same story play out:

1. A hero receives a call to adventure. This is called the inciting incident, and it's an invitation to embark on a journey that will take them out of their comfort zone and provide new challenges. Think: Innocent farm boy Luke accidentally receives a holographic message from Princess Leia pleading for help.
2. The hero refuses the call. Luke has to stay home and help Uncle Owen with the farm. Remember?
3. The hero meets a mentor. "Obi-Wan...now, that's a name I haven't heard in a long time."
4. Equipped with the mentor's training and support, they face challenges, gather allies, and transform. Luke learns from Obi-Wan, meets Han and Chewie, and together they rescue Leia and eventually defeat the Death Star.
5. And finally, they return home victorious. Luke, Leia, Han, and Chewie all receive medals for their bravery and are applauded by their friends and allies.

In your life, you star as the hero of the story. You might not get a holographic message from Princess Leia, but you will regularly face your own inciting incidents. Your call to action may involve something terrible like a job loss, a relationship ending, or the death of a loved one. Your call to adventure could take shape as the voice that nags you while trying to fall asleep at night, the general restlessness with your life, the pain in your knees and back, or those extra 25 pounds you seem to lose and regain.

These calls to action can be exciting...or off-putting. After all, inciting incidents demonstrate to the hero the flaws in their life. Like all good heroes, you'll resist the call. Your refusal could look like telling your therapist you don't need to feel your feelings, or it could be ignoring the advice to forgive...it could even be eating one more bag of Doritos! This refusal can last for a long time. It may be weeks, months, or years as you wander about trying to convince yourself everything is fine.

The journey only continues when you discover a mentor to guide you. This could be a coach, therapist, mentor, or even someone you learn from via a book like this one. Now, a lot of people see getting a mentor as the end-all-be-all step. But here's the thing: there's still one more big decision to make.

Once you have your mentor, you still have to cross the threshold into the unknown and commit to that thing you previously refused. And friend, I'll tell you...it is not fun. It can be incredibly scary to commit to the unknown, especially because you'll eventually reach a point of no return.

Whatever you were trying to avoid in your refusal of the call, it's gonna come up here. As the hero, you enter the innermost cave, where you're faced with your deepest doubts and fears. These fears are sometimes represented as a dragon and you think you need to slay the dragon. However, while in the cave, you discover that you are the dragon. And instead of slaying the dragon, you need to embrace the dragon, the fear, as a part of yourself.

Finally, the hero emerges from the cave and returns to their land to share their transformation. This metamorphosis creates hope for others facing the same obstacles the hero faced.

In fact, I went through my own hero's journey on my way to writing this book.

In December 2020, I tested positive for COVID-19. I endured weeks of exhaustion, unable to even leave the couch long enough to answer emails, and I glimpsed what the future might look like if I became unhealthier as I aged.

In the previous months, I had noticed that I was feeling really good about my life but also had a hairpin trigger on my anger. My therapist suspected the anger was stemming from some unresolved grief. I suspected that maybe I needed a new therapist because I sure didn't want to face any grief. But then I very publicly lost my job at a local housing agency, bringing up even more grief. The work at the housing authority had been hard, rewarding, and satisfying, and now it was gone.

I was also about two months into a weight loss journey. I'd made great progress at losing weight and understanding WHY I ate, but I still struggled when my therapist said I needed to learn to feel my feelings if I wanted to keep the weight off long-term.

"What do you mean feel my feelings?? Of course, I feel my feelings. Otherwise, I wouldn't be tempted to eat another brownie, drink my third whiskey, or watch the seventh hour in a row of that TV show I've seen six times," I told her. Clearly, I was feeling the feeling of exasperation! What did she know...

Little did I know it, but this conversation led to crossing the threshold for me. I got curious about what she meant. I don't like feeling confused. I want to understand what my therapist (who I'm paying good money to help me) is trying to explain. And so I started looking into this whole feeling your feelings thing.

I finally hit the point of no return when I heard about Victoria Song's work in Bending Reality. She explained emotions from her Harvard MBA, venture-capitalist perspective, explaining that when you increase your capacity to be with uncomfortable emotions instead of numbing, avoiding, diminishing, or projecting them onto others, it gives you power. Further, she reassured me that at every new level of success, you will experience new fears, so there's no point waiting until you have no fear. I had never heard anyone talk like this about feelings or emotions before –– I was much more used to people who looked like they were about to teach a yoga class being all zen and saying stupid things like "allow the discomfort." WHY would I do that!? I believed your thoughts create your feelings, so if you had a feeling you didn't like, you needed to capture the thought and change it to something that served you, right?

I was feeling huge changes, but it wasn't over yet. My approach to the innermost cave began with being tagged on a

Facebook post about a friend's certification in grief recovery. Since I had documented my journey to understand grief on Facebook, a friend made the connection. I enrolled in a seven-session process outlined in the book Grief Recovery Method to understand grief in a completely new, systematic way. I decided that if I was going to pay for assistance, maybe I needed to explore this grief thing.

For me, I had to lean into the grief recovery process while embracing what I learned from Bending Reality. When I was first learning this process, I fumbled through it. I didn't know how to imagine a problem to kind of get things going. I was just aware that I was struggling with recurring thoughts that kept bringing up the idea that "I'm not valuable." During my work with the Grief Recovery Method, I wanted to give myself an opportunity to sit with my feelings and create space to feel them.

I was really tired the first night, so I thought, "I'll go to bed early and give myself space to feel them." The next thing I knew, I was binge-watching a crime drama. The next day I had a light schedule. So in the afternoon, I went to my bedroom to "feel my feelings." Every time I tuned in to what was going on with my body, I found myself on my phone shopping, unpacking my suitcase, looking under my bed for a charger –– everything EXCEPT feeling my feelings.

That afternoon I sent a message to my Grief Recovery facilitator to ask if I could book more time the next day because I was struggling to feel anything on my own and wanted to work through the next step. She recommended I book a three-hour marathon session the next day so we could finish the process in one sitting and see it through. While that sounded terrifying, I did it. I have a firm belief that I do hard things well.

The next morning my husband was stuck on something, and he said, "I don't know what you mean by feel your feelings." So, I started walking him through the process. I was doing it right alongside him. The next thing I knew, I was curled up in a ball with his arms around me, crying my eyes out. When I finished crying, probably less than 15 minutes later, he said, "I thought you were going to tell me, not show me." Yeah, me too!

Later I went to my Grief Recovery appointment. I worked through the process as prescribed in the handbook. One of the things I like about the Grief Recovery process is that you not only process your grief, but you also learn to sit with someone processing their grief. So the facilitator and I were in two different rooms doing the worksheets separately. When I finished a certain part of the exercise, I needed to let her know so we could go over it together. I was feeling a lot of energy coursing around my body. I stood up and jumped around. I felt like shaking my hands like you are trying to fling water off them. While I was doing this, I was saying in my head over and over again, I'm not valuable. I had learned from Bending Reality that emotion is energy in motion, and I needed to finish releasing this. I told the facilitator I would be back in a moment and went for a run. I ran while repeating over and over again, I'm not valuable. When I started running, the sensation seemed like a swirl of smoke in my brain. When it finally dissipated, I stopped running and went back to finish the session. Luckily, I had already cleared a lot out and only had to run about two blocks before I was able to return to the session.

This first instance of feeling my feelings by tuning into my body was the most difficult. After this, I stopped fighting it so hard and was able to allow myself to feel much more easily. (Even so, I have still not learned to clear really hard emotions all by myself. My therapist, Anne, said it's because our body fights being in pain and being alone, so we may struggle to do this in isolation.)

And as I continued in my processing, I realized that I had experienced what most people would consider a successful life. I had been married for over 25 years, had adult kids that liked me, and was relatively financially stable (when I got fired, I was able to work on this book for over a year before I had to go back to work), but my mental chatter was way too negative for my liking. I wanted to be successful and to LIKE myself. Completing those processes created peace and a path forward, truly providing me with the reward I sought on my journey. And as my mental chatter became less and less critical, I knew I wanted to share this experience with others.

So I'm sharing it with you.

We're going to talk through everything you need to know so that you, too, can go on the hero's journey, feel your feelings, and finally live the life you want to live and ultimately feel the way you want to feel.

We'll start by talking through how these limitations get formed in us. (Surprise: it's not any kind of failing on your part, it's actually your biological wiring doing exactly what it's supposed to do!) Then, once you understand the biology of motivation, stress, and meaning-making, we'll start talking about how you can unwind the "glitchy files" that keep you stuck. And we'll actually start closing some old emotional loops together. Finally, we'll wrap up by troubleshooting some common scenarios and talking through what it looks like to live with your newly-calibrated nervous system and way of moving through the world.

Now you have a choice to make.

If you're reading this and feeling like putting this book down (or throwing it across the room), you're not alone. People often want to avoid the hero's journey or treat it as optional. Who cares if life registers as MEH. So what if you are carrying an extra 25 pounds? Maybe you are a jerk to yourself in your head. No one really has to know, right? Live an ideal life, are you kidding? That's for the likes of "those" people, you know the ones that believe personal development actually works.

The honest truth?

It's up to you.

But if you think back to that original journey we talked about, then you have a choice to make. Do you want to keep carrying that heavy bag? Or are you maybe ready to put the peanut butter down?

Here's to your journey.

CHAPTER 2
Survival - your primary motivation

Before you can effectively feel your feelings, you need to have an idea of how some feelings-related biology works –– this will help you understand the "wiring" your body has and how it plays into emotions, especially those connected to old stories or outdated coping mechanisms. We'll start out by talking through the core of human behavior: the motivational triad.

The motivational triad

How great would it be to never feel afraid? You could chase your dreams and ask for what you want. Heck, you could do anything. Right? The bad news is that's never going to happen. Your body is wired for one primary objective: to keep you alive. And fear is a key way of accomplishing that objective.

You have survived every hard thing that has happened to you up until now. You will continue to survive every hard thing that happens to you. The day you don't survive a hard thing, you won't be here to care.

Since survival is your primary function, anything your body perceives as a threat to your survival will be categorized as "bad." You might feel it as stress or fear, or pain. Your brain just sees it as a "threat." And it responds by avoiding pain, prioritizing pleasure, and conserving energy. This is called the motivational triad, and it explains a lot about human behavior. Let's look at each element in detail.

Avoiding pain

It might sound dramatic, but at the most basic level, your brain sees pain as a precursor to death. According to its logic, if pain could lead to death, you need to avoid it at all costs. And this includes all kinds of pain: physical, emotional, psychological, or spiritual. To your nervous system, the potential of battling a lion equates to battling a bully. A physical attack and a cyber-attack both lead to pain, so even though only one of those situations has the potential to actually kill you, the rudimentary classification system of your brain sorts these two attacks into the same category.

Here's the other thing that makes pain avoidance extra interesting: the "avoid pain" part of your brain is wired to prioritize the short term over the long term. So, avoiding immediate pain ranks higher than avoiding long-term pain. Eating the brownie today won't kill you, but NOT eating it today feels like pain RIGHT NOW. So you eliminate immediate pain by ignoring tomorrow's potential pain.

Similarly, lots of fear and anxiety find their root in the "avoid pain" portion of the brain. Your brain feels pain and equates that with making a mistake, and so tells you that you should stop whatever you're doing that's causing the pain because otherwise, you might DIE. We are now to the point in our evolutionary journey as a society where mild discomfort translates to pain. So we avoid any discomfort because we've come to believe it leads to death, at least in our primitive mind.

All this might sound limiting, and it is. It does serve a purpose, though. Your "avoid pain" response helps you avoid reckless risks and keeps you alive. But it introduces a constant tug-of-war between self-preservation, which your brain sees as safe, and personal growth, which it sees as risky.

Seeking pleasure

Just as your brain is wired to avoid pain, it's equally strongly motivated to seek pleasure. This involves doing what you need to do for our species to continue: seeking food, reproduction, comfort, and a group to belong to.

Historically, this pleasure-seeking motivation served as the push we needed to go out and find food in harsh conditions. While we no longer need that extra boost of motivation to go out and get the things we need to survive -- after all, food and comfort abound for many -- the drive is still there.

Similarly, we still have deep desires to belong to a group. And while food and comfort are fairly widespread and accessible, belonging seems to be in short supply. We're facing an epidemic of loneliness. While we have the opportunity to connect with people around the world, we're disconnected from ourselves and one another in dangerous ways. But the pleasure-seeking motivator remains. So we seek to satisfy our pleasure-longing by scrolling on social media, binging on Netflix, and eating endless bags of chips. So much pleasure, so little satisfaction.

Conserving energy

Your brain is also wired to conserve energy, as it wants to be sure you'll always have available resources to fight any awaiting predators and gather more food. Consider the case of exercise. Our ancestors didn't need a gym membership, a yoga class, or a daily jogging routine to stay fit. Getting food and shelter provided enough physical effort.

After my health journey of losing 30 pounds, I had to use math to understand how to maintain my weight. If my physical energy output required 1450 calories, I couldn't consume 2000 calories every day and maintain my ideal weight. But this is a modern state of being. In past millennia, if I had to hunt for berries and could only find 500 calories of berries to survive for the day, I better reduce how much energy I used.

This desire to conserve energy doesn't just apply to physical activity, though –– it also applies to mental activity. Just like your brain likes to tell you to sit on the couch, it also wants to be efficient and reduce the number of items on your conscious mind's plate. So it creates shortcuts with anything you do repetitively.

Think about how it is when you first learn to drive. You have to spend a lot of energy thinking about where to put your hands, what to do with your feet, noticing all the cars around you, the speed of your car, the signs on the road, and the other drivers' reactions. Frankly, it's exhausting. Contrast that with what it feels like when you've been driving for many years when you get in your car and go to work without hardly a thought, sometimes not even remembering how you got there. You go on auto-pilot, and your brain is happy it didn't use precious resources like conscious thought. It's the same thing with any new skill learned. When you have to use your conscious/thinking brain, it takes a lot of effort, but when you can rely on old patterns, it feels almost effortless.

Long story short? Your brain does not like working hard. It wants to solve a problem on the first try, then put the solution on autopilot. Even if the solution didn't work all that well, you at least have a familiar reference to guide you, and your brain will continue doing the same thing over and over again because it feels more efficient to use the duct-tape-and-safety-pins solution than to try a new solution. New things take a lot of energy. Using energy depletes energy reserves needed to fight imaginary lions that don't actually exist anymore.

As you embark on your hero's journey, knowing that these three survival instincts work hard to ensure you live, procreate, and conserve energy equips you with the knowledge to make choices and plans for your highest good and not just for survival.

How your stress response works

In addition to the motivational triad, your brain has some additional hardwiring called a stress reaction: you might have heard it called the fight-or-flight response. (Although that name is incomplete because you actually have three responses: fight, flight, and freeze.) This allows you to respond quickly in dangerous situations, and it's what your body defaults to in any situation that it deems to be dangerous, whether there's any real risk or not. Remember, your brain doesn't have a lot of nuance when it comes to things like this. It sees discomfort = pain = possible death. Your body chooses fight when it perceives and believes you can overpower the threat, flight when you perceive danger but believe you can avoid it by running away, and freeze when you perceive a threat but don't believe you can defeat it.

In situations that are actually dangerous, this stress response helps you stay alive. It's great for, say, surviving a lion attack. But it's not super helpful in the modern world, where you face the constant barrage of potential threats like your boss being mad at you or someone saying something negative on Facebook about you that can all feel the same to your brain as that potential lion attack.

While your stress reaction will always have the same general pattern, its severity will correlate to the degree of perceived risk for you. Telling your parents you got an F on a test is scary, but being in a car accident is way more dangerous, so you'll have a correspondingly stronger stress reaction. Now let's talk about what that fight/flight/freeze response actually looks like. The better you're able to understand the stress response in general and get a sense of how yours plays out in particular, the better equipped you'll be to access and safely feel your feelings.

In their book, *Burnout: The Secret to Unlocking the Stress Cycle*, Amelia Nagoski and Emily Nagoski explain the nervous system vividly well. If a lion chased you through the forest, you would run back to your village for safety. Returning to the village to celebrate surviving would spark the return to homeostasis. (Also called the rest and digest state, it's a balanced state in which you're relaxed and well, as opposed to a heightened state of stress.) Your feelings of excitement, exhilaration, terror, and relief would bleed off as you told the story of your narrow escape to your community. Think about when you experience a close call when driving. You breathe deeply, you express gratitude, and you may even relate the tale to a friend later at coffee. This completes the loop of the stress reaction because your brain measures the safety factor, expresses the feelings, and returns to baseline.

In modern times, you see this play out in all kinds of ways. For instance, when a child runs in front of a car, their parent screams angrily at them. The parent almost can't help sounding mad because they were scared out of their mind and reacting from a "fight" stress response. You've also probably heard stories of superhuman strength with a parent lifting a car off a child. They can thank their stress response for this. When your body thinks you're in danger, it removes all the limits that keep you from hurting yourself because it feels like your survival is at stake. In today's modern society, the times we need this superhuman strength for actual physical danger happen very infrequently. Yet, this hair-trigger system stays ready.

Now let's talk about what's actually going on in your body when you experience a stress reaction. When you perceive a threat, a part of your brain called the amygdala sounds the alarm, and the body shuts down unnecessary functions, like digestion and your immune system. It increases energy output to the parts of your body that help combat the threat, like your heart and major muscle groups. You also start breathing fast, your eyes dilate so you can see better, and stress hormones like adrenaline and cortisol jet through your body, readying your muscles for action. Adrenaline increases your heart rate, elevates your blood pressure, and boosts energy supplies. Cortisol, the primary stress hormone, increases sugars in the bloodstream, enhances your brain's use of these sugars, and increases the availability of substances that repair tissues. When the threat leaves (or you come to realize that it never really existed), your body has to go through a recovery process to return to homeostasis.

This happens because another part of your brain, called your prefrontal cortex, finally has a chance to get on board. The prefrontal cortex is where you do your executive functioning. It's the decision-making part of your brain, sometimes called the human brain or our adult self. This part of your brain can more accurately determine the validity of a threat, but it responds more slowly than the amygdala. It takes time for the threat impulse to travel up to the front of your brain and get an appropriate response.

Now, remember how we talked about your body being wired for survival and efficiency? That comes into play here, too. Because your body is actually set up to do a lot of things on auto-pilot via the autonomic nervous system. This controls involuntary and unconscious body functions, like unconscious breathing, digestion, pumping blood through your system, etc. From a survival standpoint, this setup means this part of your body keeps you alive without a lot of thought, which is great for your efficiency-loving brain. There are also two sub-parts to your autonomic nervous system: the sympathetic nervous system (SNS) and the parasympathetic nervous system (PSNS). They do different things but work in tandem. The SNS controls your body's responses to a perceived threat and the fight/flight/freeze response. The PSNS controls the rest and digest functions. This is where your body likes to spend most of its time because, again, it wants to run on autopilot and conserve energy, not go through the energy-heavy experience of fight/flight/freeze. When you experience a threat (again, real or perceived), your amygdala sounds the alarm, though, and you switch from PSNS to SNS, where you'll remain until your prefrontal cortex sends the message that the threat is not fatal and the system can reset to safety. After the adrenaline fades, you become exhausted. You need time to rest and rejuvenate.

This whole process can be seen as a "trigger-response-return to homeostasis" loop, which resembles a bell curve.

Here's the problem, though. If your brain does not get a message to return to safety, you experience an incomplete stress cycle. Your body continues to keep your SNS activated, pumping cortisol and adrenaline out to keep you on alert indefinitely. But your body isn't designed to stay in a constant state of readiness. This is exhausting and, over time, causes major health issues. Until you get the message that you're safe, you're stuck in that incomplete stress cycle, sometimes for years. (More on this in the next chapter!)

Like all the other physical processes we've talked about so far, your stress response keeps you alive and safe. But when it gets out of hand, you've got problems. Think back to the example of the woman who lifts the car off her child. That person probably knows they need to take it easy for a few days afterward and go gentle with her sore muscles for a period of time. But the same applies to the mom whose child ran in the street. The exact same hormones were pulsing through her body, and unless her body gets the message that all is well and she can proceed back to her day, she's going to stay stuck in her SNS. And unfortunately, the more your body stays in the SNS, instead of the ease-filled PSNS state of homeostasis, the more you experience dis-ease.

Our first trip to Canada: a masterclass in fight/flight/freeze responses

A few months after I began dating Barry, my now-husband, he popped the question. Well, not THE question, but the question of whether I wanted to embark on a road trip together when he went home for the summer to Canada. Naturally, my adventurous spirit screamed, "Hell yeah!" Little did I know that this journey would not only test our relationship but also provide a crash course on the various responses of the nervous system.

Somewhere in the vast expanse of Indiana, around 10 hours into our 15-hour marathon, it hits me — I'm about to meet Barry's mom for the first time. Cue my sympathetic nervous system going into overdrive. Sweaty palms, racing heart, and thoughts swirling like a tornado. I was a picture-perfect example of anxiety on wheels.

Finally, we arrived at our destination, and Barry's mom kindly offered me a steaming cup of tea. Now, here's the thing: I was not a fan of hot tea, like, at all. But I couldn't possibly turn it down. It'd be a major cultural faux pas. So I took tiny sips, prolonging the agony of consuming this liquid torment. To make matters worse, the teacup seemed to be alive, with a ceramic frog peeking out from its depths. I nearly choked on my tea, trying to figure out why a frog was photobombing my drink. Barry's mom and I shared a good laugh while my nervous system contemplated a career in slapstick comedy.

One day, in the midst of my visit, disaster struck in the shower. As I clumsily reached for my shampoo, I knocked the entire glass shelf down. Chaos ensued as shards of glass rained down on me, and my scream echoed through the house. Barry came to my rescue, and his mom, from the doorway, delivered a cringe-worthy line: "Well, I guess this isn't the first time you've seen her naked." Oh, the embarrassment! If only I could hide inside a clamshell-like a nervous system in retreat.

During my week-long stay, Barry diligently hunted for a summer job. Meanwhile, his mom regaled me with tales of the ongoing feud between Barry and his stepdad, Phil. During Barry's first semester at university, Phil had a stroke leading to him needing full-time care in a nursing home. Barry's mom lamented her decision to let him venture so far away for school. She even dropped the guilt bomb, saying, "I want you to know what I have to give up for you to be happy." Talk about a brain freeze. I responded by requesting a nap. Thank you, parasympathetic nervous system, for insisting on rest after a week of emotional roller coasters.

After an extravagant summer of phone bills, Barry decided to return to school early, and his mom bought me a plane ticket to fly up and accompany him on the drive back. Great, just great! At this point, I was juggling three jobs, burning the candle at both ends. "Tired" became my middle name, and "exhaustion" my loyal companion.

I flew in on a Friday night, hung out on Saturday, and then we set off on Sunday, with the grand plan of making it back to Arkansas in time for me to punch the clock on Monday morning.

However, just two hours away from home, Barry started to fade, struggling to keep his eyes open. He woke me up, asking for assistance in his battle against drowsiness. My response? A resounding "No way!" After all, he had spent the previous week gallivanting on vacation while I racked up 70 hours of work. While I exhibited an example of PSNS with rest, Barry drove the rest of the way, fueled by the frustration of his fight response.

Fight – Flight – Freeze

Let's go a little deeper into some of the main ways a stress response can play out so you can start to recognize them in your day-to-day. While stress responses vary from person to person and situation to situation, they tend to all boil down to the same core reactions: fight, flight, or freeze.

Fight:

Remember, fight is what your body chooses when it perceives a threat and believes it can defeat it. Whether seeing a bear in the woods or having someone yell at you at work, if you reflexively gear up, that's a fight response. It could look like Barry complaining that I wouldn't wake up and help keep him awake (since he still teases me about it 30 years later.)

Fight response can include these physical sensations:
- Tight jaw or grinding teeth
- Crying from anger
- Stomach in knots or burning
- Desire to punch, stomp, or kick
- Feeling intense anger

It may look like this response:
- Throwing a tantrum

- Resisting
- Blaming
- Complaining
- Disrupting

Flight:

Your flight response happens when your body perceives a threat and thinks it can outrun it. In the case of the bear, you'd probably literally run. In the case of a conflict at work, you might leave the room or quickly change the subject. It could look like taking a nap when your boyfriend's mom tells you about what she's giving up for your happiness.

Flight response can include these physical sensations:
- Feeling fidgety, tense, or trapped
- Excessive exercising
- Dilated, darting eyes
- Numbness in arms and legs
- Constantly moving arms, legs, feet
- Can't sit still

It may look like this response:
- Avoiding
- Denying
- Refusing
- Distracting

Freeze:

Finally, there's the freeze response, which happens when you perceive a threat and your body doesn't think you can do anything about it. In the case of the lion, you'd lay down and play dead. If your colleague yelled at you especially in the middle of an important meeting, you might dissociate, physically "freeze," or even get really tired. Or freezing in the shower so you don't get cut like I did visiting Barry's family.

Freeze response involves:
- A sense of dread
- Feeling stiff, heavy, cold, or numb
- Loud, pounding heart

- Holding your breath without realizing it
- Unable to think of a response

It may look like this response:
- Spacing out
- Going numb
- Dissociating
- Ignoring

Starting to recognize yourself in some of these responses? In the next chapter, we'll be unpacking how they can play out and be used by your body to form patterns of behavior that stick around long after they should.

Other responses:

As this book goes to print, there is a lot of discussion about other nervous system responses with very clever names like fawn, flop, flock, and Lord knows what else. I have chosen not to include any of them in THIS book for two reasons. First, I believe those are learned responses to trauma, not built into our innate survival system. What I've learned so far is they are maladaptive (we adapt and not always in a way that's healthy). Second, they aren't well researched, yet. I think in the world of the internet everyone wants to be clever and wants to coin a term. So, while they are developing, I'm watching and may update this later.

To sum up:

Understanding the motivational triad and fight/flight/freeze response helps you understand how you're wired for survival. It's all designed to keep you safe so we survive, and it serves you very well. You've survived, haven't you?

The problems start when you have a goal that conflicts with those two baseline wirings -- for instance, when you set a big goal or want to do something challenging. You may very much want to do it. But to your nervous system, it's a threat! Before you know it, your nervous system is imagining all sorts of ways things can go wrong, and it determines that the potential pain and the energetic output of a potential fight/flight/freeze aren't worth the risk. Since that is clearly in violation of the three motivations, your nervous system says, "Hard pass!" leading you to mindlessly repeat previous patterns of keeping yourself safe by avoiding potential pain, seeking extensive short-term pleasure, and allowing efficiency to run your life on autopilot...unless of course, you know how to disrupt them. We'll be getting into that shortly, but first, we need to talk about how your brain creates these "safety patterns" in response to previous threats so that you can get a sense of what some of your old patterns might be and start to see how to unravel them.

CHAPTER 3
Stress response

So far, we've mostly stuck to the underlying biology connected to feeling your feelings. You now understand why we do what we do as a species (the motivational triangle) and why we do the things we do under stress (the stress reaction of fight/flight/freeze). Now that you know the systems your body is equipped with, we can start to talk about how that oh-so-well-meaning survival impulse can end up causing issues, loading you down with old coping patterns that end up causing problems.

Your efficient filing cabinet

Remember, in the last chapter, we talked about how your stress cycles follow a pattern of trigger-response-return to homeostasis. When your brain identifies things that have caused you pain (or seem like they might cause you pain), your efficient brain wants to keep track of those trigger items to prevent future threats to survival. This all sounds great in theory, but you have to consider the frame of reference you're in when you make most of these files. Usually, you form your files when you're a child before your brain is fully developed.

Your child brain didn't have the maturity to correctly file threats or potential threats, so it had to rely heavily on your emotions to understand the world around you. You can already see how you could end up with some distorted perceptions around threats, right? Now, add the fact that when you encounter an emotion that doesn't make sense as a child, you need the adults in your life to help make sense of how to use this new information to keep you safe in the future. However, most adults in our culture have a limited amount of experience or training in how to understand and process emotions. So you add another layer of distortion to the process. That efficient "filing cabinet" where your brain keeps all the info about threats becomes like that 70 lb. bag I drug to India: effective for safety, ineffective for traveling light.

How your brain "misfiles" information about threats

Amygdala

In the last chapter we talked about the role of the amygdala and the prefrontal cortex in your stress response. (Remember, the amygdala is the part that sounds the alarm, and the prefrontal cortex is the part that figures out what's actually going on and gives the "all clear" to return to homeostasis.) The same dynamic is at play when it comes to your filing cabinet. As part of your body's efforts to reduce pain and conserve energy, your body keeps a log of potential dangers, and your amygdala is always on the lookout for anything that might tie into those. For instance, let's say your parents taught you not to talk to strangers. You log that as a threat file: strangers are a threat. And your amygdala then continually scans for anything that might play into that threat, seeing all strangers as a potential danger. Good for survival, bad for making friends.

This "filter system" acts quickly and unconsciously because your body believes that the faster you can detect danger and respond to it, the safer you'll be. When something happens to you (sometimes called a trigger), your nervous system quickly scans the system to see if this trigger suggests a similarity to another incident in your history so you can go to your fall-back response. If a similar trigger previously created pain (remember, pain leads to death), your efficient brain wants to avoid it, thus activating the fight/flight/freeze response. If you let it run wild, your amygdala's infinite ability to remember previous pain and danger and add it to the file cabinet of potential future threats will prove both frustrating and amazing. You can find yourself living a smaller and smaller life in the name of staying safe and avoiding any pain.

Prefrontal cortex

The amygdala doesn't totally run the show, though –– you also have your prefrontal cortex. Just like in your stress response, it makes the ultimate judgment calls and determines how serious a threat really is. But the information gets to your prefrontal cortex more slowly. And sometimes, you can get stuck in an open loop, with your prefrontal cortex never giving the "all clear."

Without the message to return to homeostasis, you stay in an activated state, constantly scanning for potential threats that cause pain. Plus, your prefrontal cortex is only as capable as your level of brain development, and for most people, the prefrontal cortex fully develops once they're in their early 20s. When you're making all these judgment calls about threats and potential threats as a child, you're doing it with the reasoning powers of a child. And since your sort and filter system depends on an accurate threat analysis from your brain when filing the threat away for future reference, you can start to see how a log entry may be misfiled as being more dangerous than it actually is –– hence, avoiding all strangers instead of developing a solid sense of social safety.

Sense-making: glitchy files

Another way to think about this threat assessment process is to see it as your child brain making sense of what happened. Your filing system tries to make sense of what happens to you so it can keep you safe and get your needs met in the future.

When you're a child, your brain isn't developed enough to make sense of a lot of things happening to you. Relatively innocuous things, like your parents arguing, getting grounded for bad grades, or not getting invited to a sleepover, could all be things you can't make sense of, depending on your age, when they happen. When these things occur, your body gets flooded with unpleasant sensations. And remember, to your brain, unpleasant sensations = pain = death, so your brain wants to make sense of these sensations and assign them a pattern and a threat level so you can avoid feeling them ever again.

Now ideally, your parents help you with making sense of the world you don't understand, but that doesn't always happen. The adults in your life can exacerbate the pain by not knowing how to help you make sense of it and reestablish equilibrium. They might tell you to shake it off or ignore those people and what they think. At the absolute worst, they might minimize the pain as not a big deal. In the adult world, it's not a big deal to not get invited to a sleepover and feel rejected. But little kids' brains don't yet have the experience to understand that.

Even though you can't make sense of this pain, your efficient brain assigns meaning: it labels the "file" you're experiencing from your perspective at the time: that of a little kid. This means you end up assigning meanings like "there's something wrong with me" or "I don't belong in the group."

This meaning-making gets intensified when you look to the adults in your life for assistance, and they let you down. This usually doesn't happen intentionally. Many of us didn't have emotionally attuned parents because, quite frankly, society did not encourage people to understand and talk about their feelings and emotions. We have come a long way in the last 40 years in understanding brain development, emotional intelligence, and impacts on the nervous system, so the truth is, most of our parents were doing the best they could and repeating what they had been taught.

Consider the case of crying. When you're an infant, crying works to get your needs met (and, from your brain's perspective, your pain alleviated.) Infants cry to get food, change their diapers, and be held. As you get older, your crying may become less effective. Many of us were told, "Stop crying, or

I'll give you something to cry about." Once you hear that, your little kid brain often translates that into a file that says, "Emotions are bad. Avoid them at all costs."

I slightly evolved because I told my children, "You are allowed to cry as long as it's in any room I'm not in," which means that my kids' nervous systems likely heard, "If you feel emotions, go be alone, and face whatever lion might come at you by yourself."

Now, as an adult, telling a child to go to their room to cry would barely register as noteworthy by the end of the day. But as you now know, a child's amygdala and prefrontal cortex will to get to work making meaning so they can feel safe. And over time, all that sense-making leads to an extensive log of files designed to keep you safe.

"Don't talk to strangers

Don't touch hot stoves

Don't hang around the wrong crowd

Don't be different

Don't cry, or I'll give you something to cry about"

Most of these log entries were created when you had sensations in your body you couldn't make sense of, triggered by your fight or flight response. The trauma in and of itself isn't so much the problem as the lasting effects those glitchy files can have on your worldview if you're unaware of them.

Let's look at an example. Let's say your dad is trying to help you with your math homework, and you aren't getting it. Your dad gets really frustrated and yells at you. You may start to cry, which then makes him madder. Your little kid brain can make this mean any number of things: I'm stupid, there's something wrong with me, I don't deserve love, and crying makes everything worse. You don't yet know that there's a whole world out there which doesn't revolve around you. But if your parents aren't tuned in to how much this upsets you, you're left in this pain alone with only your little kid's experience level to assign meaning. It can shape our identity and even affect our posture by keeping us always ready to protect ourselves. And if you use your childhood experiences to mean there's something wrong with you, this will form your worldview, affecting your decisions without you even realizing it. These mislabeled files can keep you stuck for a really long time.

Now, contrast this experience with learning to ride a bike. When you learn to ride a bike, you probably started out afraid to fall. Then you tried it, fell, cried, then your body saw you didn't die from the pain. You also likely had an older human encouraging you to try again and telling you that you would get it eventually. So you tried again and maybe fell again. Your brain noticed that you made it a bit further on your second attempt, and the pain from the first fall had already subsided. It made sense of the pain and revised the file to be "perseverance pays off" instead of "bike = pain = death." You can do this same kind of revising with the emotional files your mind forms as long as you know they're there. But so many of us get "stuck" with old files.

When I talk to adults about their fear of public speaking, they often tell me a story from 7th grade where they messed up speaking. Their classmates laughed, felt sensations, and labeled them as embarrassment. They made it mean speaking is bad. Their threat assessment process determined that future speaking opportunities were very high risk. Despite the ill effects this may have on their career, they hold tight to the file in the filing cabinet. You may have heard the joke that people would rather be in the coffin than give a eulogy because fear of death ranks second to fear of public speaking. To understand why things like this become so heightened, you need to add another layer to your understanding of the motivational triad.

Abandonment and getting stuck

Your brain views belonging to a group (family, community, couple, etc.) in at least two important ways: (1) social relationships contribute to our seeking pleasure motivation, and (2) surviving (aka seeking pleasure, avoiding pain, and conserving energy) is easier when you're part of a group.

When you are excluded from a group or feel like you're at threat of being excluded, your little kid brain can make this pain mean that you could die. After all, if you're alone, you may have to face the lion alone. No village to protect you, no one to tell your stories of escape to, and no one to celebrate with. Losing the attachment to your group causes a very heightened sensation your brain doesn't know how to make sense of. This loss of attachment is called abandonment. Abandonment can look different for each of us. It could be physical abandonment like divorce, death, or even an older sibling going off to college. It could be emotional, like a parent who is emotionally unavailable because of their own issues or moving to a new school because your parents got a new job and you lose your friends.

Some of these things are a natural part of life, and with the consistent love of your family, you can develop the resilience to weather these storms. If the adults in your life help you accurately make sense of what happens, then you may not file the messages as pain = death. But if you don't receive that support, comfort, or even acknowledgment, you can become overwhelmed by the intensity of the need to be comforted. You may also decide there must be something wrong with you if no one wants to meet your needs or stay with you. This creates a cycle of shame. If you want something or are a bother, something must be wrong with you. If abandonment overloads your nervous system like this, you may find yourself ill-equipped to complete a stress cycle and return to homeostasis. This leaves your nervous system activated in a perpetual fight/flight/freeze state, where your amygdala is constantly on alert. When you're in this kind of situation, even just existing in your body can feel unsafe.

If you're constantly feeling uncomfortable sensations in your body, and you can't make sense of them, your brain will often begin to ignore those emotions as a way to keep you safe. You may inadvertently abandon yourself in the name of surviving. As you get older, you may numb these feelings with food, alcohol, sex, shopping, or trying to escape reality. Then you often compound the pain by beating up on yourself about overeating, getting drunk, overspending, or binging on Netflix.

As adults, we often don't see how this tendency to abandon ourselves and ignore our physical sensations lead to the issues we desperately want to change about ourselves: procrastination, imposter syndrome, anger issues, depression, and many others. We also don't see how these ignored sensations with the mislabeled files shape our beliefs about ourselves and how the world works. You might think you need to try harder, think better, do more, or else numb yourself to the sensations. Now, of course, all that takes a lot of work. You need someone to manage it all.

Enter: the inner critic

This file cabinet of "glitchy files" needs a manager. Your original manager is our inner child. The inner child who simply wants to be loved wants to trust others and for everyone to be happy. Over time, your brain may decide that the inner child doesn't have enough backbone to keep you safe. So you develop your inner critic as a defense mechanism. The inner critic has one role: to ensure all these log entries of danger are kept ready to protect you. The inner critic begins to help us develop tools for safety.

Dr. Bessel van der Kolk, author of *The Body Keeps Score* and trauma researcher for 50 years, explains that when we experience trauma, we may decide taking on the perpetrator as a voice in our head can serve as a protective measure. Like if that person lives in our head, they can keep the pain from ever happening again. This is faulty thinking, but it's similar to noticing how bullied kids often try to gain power over their lives by bullying someone smaller than them.

These different parts begin to form a committee in your head, wrestling for control. The inner child continues to trust people who aren't safe in a desperate search for love and belonging. The inner critic develops tools that it feels are more effective, like perfectionism, judgment, and holding people at arm's length to try to protect you from the hurt you experienced as a child.

If your inner critic could protect you, then the inner child might possibly be able to receive love. But getting close enough to people to receive love seems incredibly dangerous to the inner critic. So your inner critic wants to hide your inner child. Deep, deep, deep, deep away. It's like the scene in National Treasure. You have to enter through the crypt, pull out the coffin, crawl inside the tomb, find a way down the rickety elevator that breaks, then down the wobbly, shaky stairs. You find the room that looks like it used to be full of treasure, but it is empty. You see there's one more door that would allow you to explore the depths of your heart. You're too afraid of putting the key into the hole and unlocking the door. You've believed the lie that there's something wrong with you for so long it's too painful to think of knowing yourself. You certainly don't let others in. You can't because you can't go in yourself. If other people got into the deepest recesses of your heart, they would find out how truly awful you are, they would leave you, and you would surely die.

So you either never go into the deep areas of your heart, or if you do, you content yourself to play in the empty treasure room and believe it's enough. Your inner child desperately wants to convince you that it's OK to trust again. It's OK to play again. It's OK to allow others into the treasure room that is your heart. Your inner critic wants to protect you at all costs. It will develop tools it deems necessary for survival, like self-judgment and perfectionism.

Self-judgment and perfectionism

Judgment is an opinion or conclusion based on available material. As a little kid, your available material is limited. You begin to believe if you can be good enough if you can do the right thing, if you could just say the right thing, then maybe you could stay out of trouble. Maybe people wouldn't leave you. Maybe the world would be safe. All of this leads to perfectionism, which is rooted in shame. Shame tells you that something must be wrong with you; otherwise, people wouldn't leave you or want to hurt you.

As you become an adult, your inner critic comes to believe that the only effective protection is to crack the whip. If it can keep you running harder and faster, it can potentially protect you. This is exhausting and leads to all sorts of negative outcomes. That's why many people try to kick their inner critic to the curb as soon as they become aware of it. But this does them a disservice. Your inner critic has been doing its job very well. It has been keeping you safe. It has been watching out for your survival. And if you try to just kick it to the curb, it's not really going to be super effective. Number one, doing that is scary because you feel like you're ditching all the protective tools that you have. Number two, it just doesn't work because the inner critic will fight kicking and screaming because your brain has hired it as the manager of the glitchy files.

The truth is, things won't change unless you're able to complete those emotional cycles and relabel those files. Once you do that, there's no real need for a manager, and you'll often find that the inner critic becomes much quieter without you having to do much about them. The way you get there is by feeling those emotions you're afraid to feel so your body can get that all-clear signal to go back to homeostasis. And that's what we'll start getting into in chapter four.

To sum up:

By now, you can see your nervous system and body are doing the best they can with the tools they have and the maturity you had when you created your files. Like my 70-pound suitcase, the subconscious information stored to alleviate our fears may not contribute to our well-being. It just helps us keep surviving. Let's uncover how this bag got packed, to begin with, so you can understand how your brain assigned meaning to those files and learn how to unpack it without judging yourself.

CHAPTER 4
Toxic waste of beliefs

So far, we've seen how your brain assigns meaning to things in an effort to make sense of the world and keep you safe. And that's the keyword: safe. These meaning-making efforts don't particularly promote a courageous, well-designed life because that's not their priority. And, when you practice them enough over time, these thought patterns become entrenched beliefs. They might feel like the truth rather than a thought pattern you choose to entertain. After all, you've had them for a long time. You formed them as a child as a way to understand the world and survive.

But many of those beliefs no longer serve you when you consider going for your dreams and goals. Some of them create more problems than they solve and more risks than they mitigate. There are several common beliefs that get planted in childhood as a way to make sense of the world. We're going to unpack them together -- but first, let's take a look at what beliefs are so you can start to regain some conscious control over yours, and then walk through some of the most common patterns of negative beliefs, so it becomes easier for you to spot them and unpack them.

What are beliefs?

A belief is a thought you've had so many times it seems like the truth. By THE truth, I mean it is how you see the world. Literally, your worldview. They tend to form when you're a child, and lots of people come to a reckoning with those beliefs later in life. In keeping with our metaphor so far, beliefs usually form out of several similar files -- and once they come together, they're hard to shake! I've observed many college students and young adults struggle to reconcile what they've always been taught and believed with the new information they encounter in college. This seems to be an especially big shift in those of us from small towns and lower socio-economic backgrounds because we may not have been exposed to many different ideas growing up. Or we're often taught that things are different than we were led to believe. For instance, certain things we might have been taught are wrong or bad simply aren't.

Much like the individual "files" your brain develops for safety, your beliefs are developed with efficiency in mind. That's why these early childhood beliefs tend to be fairly simple and black and white. Many important ideas are nuanced and take thoughtful consideration. But when you're under threat from a lion, thoughtful consideration is the last thing you need. This is also why your brain hangs onto these beliefs for so long. It takes energy to shift a worldview, and your brain is wired to conserve energy, so it's easier to just accept what you already believe. The problem arises when those beliefs stop serving you. For instance, as we talked about earlier, "Don't talk to strangers" is a good belief to keep you from being kidnapped as a child. But it's not helpful when you're grown up and trying to make friends. In fact, it can cause a lot of loneliness.

Sometimes we even form beliefs for our parents' brain's efficiency. For instance, if you're constantly told to "quit asking for things," your parents don't have to think about if they have the capacity to do whatever you want them to do. My son, Josh, got a degree in Supply Chain Management, which he chose because he had been practicing it for many years on me. He figured out early on that his busy, workaholic mom would say no to any activities in his social life if she had to work out the logistics. If he could work out all the details in advance and all he needed was a driver, I would say yes. Around 14, I would get a request like this. "Mom, can I go to the movies?" I would hesitate. He would follow it up with, "I'll go home with Trey after school. His mom will pick up the girls and take us to the movies. After the movie, can you take everyone home? The movie should be over by 9:30?" My only reason for saying no would involve admitting I was too lazy to get out at 9:30 at night. He made it really hard to say no to such an easy request.

Josh learned how to work around me, and you probably learned how to work around your parents too. But what about those times when you couldn't get the workaround? What about when you're told "no?" This tends to lead to unpleasant emotions flooding through your body. When you're young and don't know what to do with those emotions, you assign meaning to them, forming your beliefs. For instance, if you had a parent like me, who didn't want to work out the logistics, and you got told "no," you might have developed the belief that you shouldn't ask for anything because it's not safe. This makes new job interviews, sales calls, and even dating much harder.

Here's the tricky part though: you probably aren't consciously aware of this belief. It masquerades as other things, like "I don't like asking for help," "I don't want to bother them," or "I'm probably not the right fit." Do you see how this could be detrimental to asking for your needs to be met at work and in relationships? The extra twist on top is something called confirmation bias –– our brains love to be right. In fact, there's a part of your brain called the reticular activating system, which only notices things that confirm you're right ––it's why you notice all the blue Hondas after you buy one.

Similarly, if you have a latent belief that people are out to get you, you'll notice the people who do cause problems for you, and you won't notice when other people are being helpful. You'll think it's either a one-off, or you won't even pay attention to the evidence disputing your belief because it doesn't feel safe to gather evidence contrary to what you believe. Remember, your brain is wired for survival and efficiency. If you already have an ingrained response pattern to something (even if it doesn't work all that well), why would you change it? That's inefficient from the brain's perspective.

This becomes really challenging because these beliefs become the lens through which all your experiences are scanned. If they confirm the belief, they're legitimized. If they don't confirm the belief, they're ignored. You build up years of "proof" confirming your belief while ignoring evidence to the contrary. By the time you're grown, you accept this belief system as gospel truth.

Now these beliefs might not affect you in your day to day. If you're working in an area where you know what you're doing, feel comfortable, and know all the players and all the expectations, you do just fine. But when things get tricky, those beliefs come to the surface. See how you behave when you move into a new role, relationship, business, or situation where you don't feel safe and comfortable, and notice how different it is from your day-to-day!

Eventually, you may realize that you want more out of your life, and you'll start to see the limits that those beliefs put on you –– just like my husband did when co-worker tried to teach him the computer shortcut to do a screen capture by pressing Windows key + Shift key + S key at the same time. For most people, this is no problem. But my husband found it almost impossible to do. What he didn't realize until later was that his pinkie actually didn't have the flexibility to do that move. My husband, Barry, broke his left pinkie in high school. The docs did their best to set it but didn't bother with an X-ray. When the cast came off after 6 weeks, his pinkie was totally immobile and stuck at a wonky 90-degree angle. They wanted to re-break it, but summer break was looming, and Barry didn't want to be cast-bound again. So, his crooked pinkie became a lifelong companion.

Now, Barry's a seasoned programmer, and most of the time, that little finger serves him just fine for hitting the shift key. It doesn't slow him down much. But recently, when his co-worker tried to enlighten him about a screen capture shortcut: Windows key + Shift key + S. Cue the complaints! He grumbled about this silly shortcut being next to impossible. That's when I chimed in with a playful jab, "Hey, Adobe's got shortcuts with 3-4 keys galore!"

As Barry attempted the finger dance, he realized his inflexible pinkie posed a real challenge. It was like playing Twister with his hand, all odd angles and contortions. I think our emotions can be just like Barry's stubborn pinkie. Most of the time, they're fine and dandy. But sometimes, we need that flexibility to truly be ourselves, to let our emotions flow freely and unhindered.

Toxic waste: when old beliefs cause you to get stuck

Now that's all well and good, right? You find out that you have a limiting belief, and you say, "Hey, I don't want that anymore!" and you change it. Unfortunately, it's not quite that simple. Because while Barry can easily see the odd angle in his finger, your brain likes to keep uncomfortable feelings and the "files" they create out of sight, out of mind. This can make it hard to see the beliefs that are holding you back.

And, if your mind has decided to simply eliminate feeling pain as part of its desire for efficiency, you can actually get stuck in the middle of that trigger-response-return to homeostasis curve we've talked about, remaining activated for years. If you imagine the trigger-response-return as a bell curve, the unexpressed emotion grinds to a stop at the top of the curve when it feels unsafe to process the rest of the emotions, getting stuck in the "response" section. The emotional loop is unable to complete, leaving you stuck.

Initially, these instances may just stack up in your mind like clutter in a house. It might work for a while, but eventually, you'll have to clear that desk off. What would happen if you tried to clear your desk by burying your clutter in the backyard, like factories used to do with toxic waste? This is what your unconscious mind tends to do with all that clutter.

In The Body Keeps Score, Dr. van der Kolk shares extensive evidence that even though you may not consciously remember things that happened to you, your body can still contain these incomplete cycles, even if they happened a long time ago. You don't feel like they should have any impact on today. Like toxic waste, when different types of toxic material interact together, unpredictable reactions occur.

Over time, your brain may create barrels -- aka beliefs -- for you to dump trash in to make it easier for you to get rid of the incomplete cycles more efficiently. Your haphazard filing system trips the alarm bells if anyone gets near a buried barrel. That barrel contains a whole lot of hurt, and you're wired to avoid pain.

Of course, none of this is visible from the outside. We think the barrels remain safe and sound, buried deep beneath the surface. And we tell ourselves all kinds of things to avoid these barrels.

"Quit dwelling on the past"

"Don't blame your parents for everything"

"Suck it up, buttercup."

But the pain still leaks out around the edges. You might try to numb it with food, alcohol, or binging on screens. Each time something happens to make you feel like that again, you get triggered because you unconsciously feel unsafe. More numbing is required.

Like all the other things your brain does, this is not inherently bad. It serves a purpose: to keep you safe so you can survive. Remember, you're wired to avoid pain and find pleasure in the most efficient way possible. But you have bigger aspirations for your life than survival. And that's where the barrels start to get in the way. Until you feel the feelings in the barrels and complete those incomplete cycles, they will hold you back.

I tried to ignore this truth for a long time. As a positive-thinking evangelist, I preached that your beliefs create your thoughts, and your thoughts create your feelings. I practiced replacing beliefs. However, despite all my positive thinking, it seemed nagging negative thoughts continued to hound me. I preferred to think of new thoughts than to process my feelings. Whenever I felt unpleasant feelings, I just decided that I needed to think better, more positively, or something. Despite my best efforts, I still got angry very easily, mainly when confused, and especially if someone didn't follow my instructions. I would review in my mind what I had said. I often talked to the person about what they heard and why the two didn't match. Then after the frustration faded, I would be very upset that I had been so confused and sounded angry. The confusion and anger amplified if you put me in a situation where I didn't feel confident.

During my tenure at the housing authority, I definitely had to apologize more times than I care to remember because I didn't treat people in alignment with my character because of momentary frustration. I didn't even realize how much I had disrespected one of my most trusted team members until someone had the courage to call me out. While I'm proud of the level of vulnerability I showed by apologizing to this person in front of the team, I couldn't figure out why I acted the way I did when I was stressed out.

I didn't realize how constantly activated my nervous system was, and was unaware of all the open loops of emotions. Then when I started trying to feel my feelings, I thought it meant I had to tell you this thing happened, as in, "I felt like XYZ." I also didn't have this definition of emotions being sensations in my body. I skipped the step of allowing the emotion to give me information before assigning meaning to my thoughts to create my feelings.

Seven common belief barrels

Part of the work of starting to feel your feelings is being able to put names on the barrels of beliefs you might have festering beneath the surface. In my coaching work, I tend to see the same seven over and over again. Review the next sections and see if you spot any familiar beliefs. Remember, they may only surface when you're stressed or try to stretch beyond your comfort zone, like when you attempt to set a new goal. Noticing these ideas can begin to help your amygdala become more efficient in filing threats correctly (instead of just relying on old patterns). It can help your prefrontal cortex decide the fight/flight/freeze response unnecessarily triggered, so it's OK to go back to rest and digest.

I'm not lovable

Synonyms include: repulsive, unpleasant, irritable, loathsome, hateful, abhorrent, dreadful, awful, offensive

The belief of not being lovable often finds its roots in various experiences and messages you've encountered throughout your life. It's possible that not achieving perfect grades led you to believe you weren't good enough or deserving of love. Experiencing a breakup where your partner quickly moved on to someone else may have intensified this belief, making you question your worthiness of love and companionship. Additionally, growing up in a family dynamic where you felt overshadowed by a favored sibling or not receiving equal attention and affection could have reinforced the belief that you are not lovable. Furthermore, significant losses or abandonment by someone important in your life can also contribute to this belief.

The belief that "I'm not lovable" can manifest in various ways. It might lead you to reject the love others offer, believing they would not truly accept you if they knew the real you. Alternatively, it can manifest as codependency and people-pleasing, where you go to great lengths to gain the love and approval of others. However, paradoxically, when someone does express love towards you, you may find yourself pushing them away, fearing abandonment or rejection. This may lead you to believe it's better to leave before they have the chance to abandon you.

In my own personal experience, I endured three separate episodes of sexual abuse before entering college. As a result, I associated love with sex, leading me to engage in risky behaviors in an attempt to fulfill my core need for love.

I don't belong

Synonyms include: disconnect, disassociate, oppose, refuse, different, avoid

The belief of not belonging can stem from various experiences and situations that make you feel excluded or rejected. It can be as simple as getting made fun of, being called a name, or feeling left out of certain social circles, such as being unable to sit at the "right" table during lunch. Although these may not seem like significant events, they can quickly trigger your innate need for belonging. Our brains are wired to perceive isolation as a threat to survival as if we were alone and vulnerable against lions in the wild. This primal instinct is vividly portrayed in the cafeteria scene in Mean Girls, where the characters' sense of belonging is clearly depicted.

The belief that "I don't belong" can manifest in various ways. You may struggle to feel comfortable in your own skin as if you don't truly fit in or belong anywhere. Even when surrounded by friends or in social settings, you might still experience a sense of isolation and detachment. It may feel like there is no specific place or group where you truly belong. In some cases, people may physically display signs of feeling small and invisible, such as hunching their shoulders, keeping their heads down, or avoiding eye contact.

I am not enough/I'm not good enough

Synonyms include: incompetent, inadequate, unsatisfactory

This belief that you are not enough is rooted in comparing yourself to others. It may come from situations where you have an older sibling who excels in school or sports, or perhaps you felt inadequate because you don't get to wear the latest trendy clothes, didn't win a spelling bee, or didn't make a sports team. It's important to recognize that this belief may not stem from a single incident but can be shaped by an entire childhood filled with constant feelings of falling short, no matter how hard you try.

This belief can show up in various ways in your life. It may lead to a sense of hopelessness, creating the belief that life will never be any different or better for you. You may easily become upset when others insinuate or imply that you are not enough, as their remarks confirm your deepest fears and insecurities. Furthermore, this belief can affect your ability to set and maintain healthy boundaries. You may find it challenging to assert your needs and stand up for yourself, as the belief of not being enough undermines your self-worth and confidence. You may have been told you should know better.

I'm not valuable

Synonyms include irrelevant, cheap, useless, unimportant, or worthless

The belief that you are not valuable can originate from various sources, extending beyond the realm of money, although financial considerations often become tangled up with it. This belief can arise from experiences of literal physical abandonment, such as when someone important to you leaves, leading you to interpret their departure as a sign that you are disposable or unworthy of love and connection. Additionally, if you have been repeatedly told that you are useless, will never amount to anything, or consistently receive messages that diminish your value, it can reinforce the belief that you lack worth. For instance, if your parents consistently spent money on buying nice clothes for your brother while you only got his hand-me-downs, it can contribute to feelings of inadequacy and reinforce the belief that you are not deserving of equal treatment.

This belief can show up by not being willing to invest in yourself, not taking care of health issues that arise, or being afraid to pursue your dreams, especially if they cost money. You may also spend excessive amounts of money on your children to overcompensate for the lack you felt as a child. You may also allow others to treat you poorly because they are confirming the belief that you aren't valuable, so this feels safe and comfortable.

This belief can be extra difficult if you perceive that society seems to classify you as irrelevant or not contributing in monetary ways, as so often happens with women. As I once said to Barry, I contribute in ways beyond the amount of money I deposit into the checking account!

I'm not worthy

Synonyms include: unreliable, inappropriate, ineligible, shameful, undeserving, unfit

Closely tied to not being valuable, which is more about usefulness and contribution, worthiness is more about your intrinsic quality as a human. Throughout your life, you may have encountered situations where you were made to feel that you should be grateful for what you have or that you don't deserve anything better. These messages might have been conveyed through experiences such as losing privileges due to not following family rules. Although your parents may have intended to teach you respect and accountability, you may have internalized it as a belief of "not worthy."

The belief of "I'm not worthy" can manifest in various ways. It can be seen in your difficulty accepting compliments, feeling uncomfortable when receiving recognition for your achievements, or engaging in self-sabotaging behaviors. These behaviors may stem from a deep-rooted belief that you are not deserving of the positive attention or success that comes your way.

This belief can create a barrier to fully embracing and accepting the love, support, and recognition that others offer you. It can hinder your ability to acknowledge your own worth and value, leading to a reluctance to receive compliments or acknowledge your own accomplishments. The notion of not being worthy can permeate your thoughts and actions, preventing you from fully embracing your true potential and experiencing the joy and fulfillment that come with self-acceptance and self-worth.

I don't trust myself

Synonyms include: doubt, distrust, uncertainty, disbelief

The belief of not trusting yourself can come from various scenarios, often stemming from mistakes that seem to have dire consequences. For instance, forgetting to turn in a permission slip for a field trip, losing a cherished piece of jewelry your grandma gave you, or choosing the wrong friends who ultimately took advantage of you. Additionally, not trusting yourself can emerge when you fail or make mistakes and then beat up on yourself. You literally create a lack of safety inside ourselves. Life gets infinitely harder when you believe you can't trust yourself, as it undermines your confidence in your own abilities.

Furthermore, this lack of self-trust can also arise from experiencing trauma and wishing you had reacted differently, such as fighting back. Even if freezing was the safest response in that situation, you might still doubt your own judgment and actions. The problem lies in how we remember these events and the meaning we attach to them, often engaging in self-blame and dwelling on what we shoulda, woulda, coulda done differently.

The belief of not trusting yourself can manifest in various ways throughout your life. It may lead to being overly cautious in forming new friendships, fearing that others may take advantage of you again. This lack of self-trust can also result in difficulty making decisions, as you constantly worry about making the wrong choice and disappointing others. Even simple things like the "Where should we go for dinner?" conversations are fraught with imagined negative consequences. Additionally, not trusting yourself can create reluctance in taking on leadership roles. If you lack confidence in leading yourself, it becomes difficult to envision others following you. The belief that you cannot trust your own abilities and decisions diminishes your self-perception and undermines your leadership potential. It erodes the belief that you have something valuable to offer and can make a meaningful impact.

I don't have what it takes

Synonyms include: inept, stupid, powerless, unsuitable, weak, unqualified, incompetent

The belief of not having what it takes often takes root in subtle ways, shaped by experiences such as not making a sports team, not being chosen for the desired role in a school play, or not getting a chance to start in a sport. Additionally, the disappointment reflected in your parents' expressions when you made a mistake could have contributed to burying these feelings deep within. Perhaps your parents had unrealistic expectations for your age and skill level, or comparisons to other family members who excel in areas where you struggle may have left you feeling inadequate.

As time goes on, these buried emotions and self-doubts manifest in different aspects of your life. You find yourself holding back from pursuing your dreams, not applying for a job unless you meet every single qualification, and feeling afraid to embark on a new side hustle. The fear of failure and the uncertainty you don't measure up can create a barrier that prevents you from taking risks and embracing new opportunities.

Furthermore, this belief can also manifest as a fear of failure or even a fear of success. The fear of failure stems from the worry that you won't meet your own or others' expectations, while the fear of success stems from the uncertainty of handling the responsibilities and changes that come with achieving your goals.

How these beliefs play out in your life

You might already be getting a sense of what some of your negative beliefs are. Let's talk about some of the subtle ways these beliefs can influence your life. Take the example of me learning how to ride a bike.

For most of my adult life, I didn't think I could really ride a bike because when I rode, my knees hurt really bad even after a few miles. I had always just bought bikes at garage sales for $25 since I couldn't ride very far anyway. While raising my kids, it wasn't a big deal that I couldn't ride a bike far.

Negative belief: I'm not valuable, so why spend money on a quality bike?

In my early 40s, my best friend started dating this new guy with a keen interest in bikes, both motorcycles and bicycles. His contagious passion for biking had me telling him about my sad knees. He saw my bike and said, "It's no wonder you don't love to ride. C'mon, let's go look at bikes." We went to our local bike shop, where he picked a bike out, took me to the parking lot, and said, "Here, try this." Super skeptical because the parking lot was on a hill; I tried it so I didn't look like a baby in front of my friend's new boyfriend. Shockingly, my knees didn't hurt. He explained that my old bike weighed a lot and didn't have the proper equipment to make it an easier ride. I fell in love with biking but still mentally restricted how far I could ride at a time. After just 5-7 miles, I would quit to prevent overexertion and being in pain for several days.

Negative belief: I am not enough, so I have to stop before I hurt myself!

At the time, this didn't seem like a problem. One fall, I joined a group that met weekly to ride the 5.5-mile path around Lake Fayetteville for a few months. As long as I could make it around once, I could still be part of the group. Who cares if I can't ride more than 5 miles at a time?

Negative belief: I don't belong, but maybe I can pretend to be part of the group.

A few years later, some trails near our house were completed. My husband suggested I ride my bike to work with the trail access. I haughtily replied, "I ride my bike for recreation, not transportation." My brain did not hear the word "not." From then on, I would drive different ways to work, trying to figure out the way with the fewest hills, the least amount of time on the road, and the least amount of effort to use my bike as transportation. Look how my brain wanted to avoid pain, increase pleasure, and be efficient! A few Saturdays later, I asked if we could ride from home to the Farmer's Market because it would take us right by my work. He agreed, and I shocked myself by taking the 8.5-mile ride with plenty of energy to enjoy the market. After riding home, I still had the stamina for the rest of the day, maybe even more than normal.

Even after I started riding, there were certain hills that I would go around believing I couldn't possibly ride up them. *Negative belief: I don't have what it takes, so why try.*

During the pandemic, I received a hazard pay bonus. My growing confidence made me consider the idea of a lighter bike with better performance for commuting.

Shifting belief: Maybe I'm finally worthy. I've proven I can ride consistently.

Eventually, I started riding my bike to work. Over the next few months, I would find a way in every conversation to share a tidbit about riding my bike to work. If anyone said, "How are you?" I would say, "I'm fine, not tired, even though I ride my bike to work. Yeah, it's no big deal. It's only 8.5 miles. Oh yeah, no sweat, it's around 45 minutes." I totally took on the identity of "I'm a cyclist commuter."

As I look back over my 10-year evolution as a biker, I can see how overcoming this physical limitation also grew my mental stamina and belief in myself. I could literally point to a hill and say when I first started riding my bike, I walked that hill. But over time, I gradually developed my skills to be able to ride up it slowly, then faster and faster with less effort.

54 Toxic waste of beliefs

This effort of learning to feel your emotions and replace limiting beliefs is similar. Start slowly, be kind to yourself, and give it time. You'll keep getting better and better.

To sum up:

Your brain and body are wired for survival, and they're very effective at assigning meaning to the things that happen to you because that will keep you safe. That's good for survival but not so much for anything else. If you want to live your life to the fullest, then you have to be able to get at those beliefs and shift them. The good news is, your beliefs don't happen "to you;" they're just misfiled info from a well-meaning brain. The problem arises when they get ignored, stuck, and buried deep within you like toxic waste. To shift any belief, you have to feel whatever stuck feelings you may have around it. This, of course, starts with awareness of what your negative beliefs might be and how they might be playing out in your life. You've seen an example of how mine come into play, so you're probably starting to spot some in your own life too, which is great –– because now we're going to start talking about how to feel your feelings and shift them!

CHAPTER 5
Emotions to guide the way

By now, you're probably thinking, "OK, I got it. I have a problem. Now what do I do with it?"

The first thing I'm going to invite you to do is reframe that notion. The thought, "I have a problem," comes from a place of shame, like there's something wrong with you. This is not true. You've survived everything that's happened to you so far, and done so beautifully. Your body is doing exactly what it's wired to do in keeping you alive. So it's not that there's something wrong with you. It's just that you want something different now. That heavy suitcase, those barrels of beliefs that have helped you survive, will hold you back from accomplishing your goals.

I want to share with you the freedom I've experienced by allowing my body the time and space to complete cycles from past pain. I want you to have the chance to unpack the suitcase to determine if you really need to continue to protect yourself in the same ways or if there are new techniques you can use to create safety for yourself. Remember, toxic waste disposed of properly ceases to be harmful. Your barrels of beliefs can be processed to remove the toxicity. That's what we're going to start moving towards now. We'll talk about how you can create the sense of safety your nervous system needs to close any loops that got stuck open, so you can start processing your emotions and move forward.

The first step? Learning how to work with your emotions, understanding your motivational style, and getting a sense of your window of tolerance.

What are emotions?

It sounds like kind of a crazy question...after all, you feel emotions all day long! You know what sadness, anger, happiness, or contentment feels like. But what are they, really?

Emotions are real-time data sparked by sensations in the body. They can be measured by a machine or observation because they are bodily reactions activated through neurotransmitters and hormones released by the brain. Victoria Song describes them as energy in motion. Now you'll note, so far, the emotions don't have any meaning assigned to them. They're just sensations.

When you put a meaning to an emotion, it becomes a feeling. For instance, if you experience a sensation in your body when your teacher asks you a question, and you stutter, making the whole class laugh, you might label that sensation as joy because you love the attention and love making people laugh. Or you might label it as embarrassment because you hate the attention and hate people laughing at you. It's the same sensation, the same emotion. The thinking brain assigns meaning to it, and then it becomes a feeling.

Feelings are the conscious experience of emotional reactions. They can be more biased and altered by mental interpretations. They aren't recorded by machines. Instead, they are measured by self-reporting tools like interviews, surveys, and assessments.

Finally, because your feelings are tied in with the thinking mind, which is also the part of you making those glitchy files, sometimes things can get twisted up. This is how unhealthy coping skills develop. Remember, your brain loves shortcuts, so if you're in a situation where something happens and then is immediately followed by a certain action, your brain may link the two. For instance, sometimes parents attempt to help you make sense of your pain by introducing different coping strategies which have worked for them. "Honey, you felt left out at school? Here, have a cookie." Your brain now has crossed-wired the idea, "If you feel pain, seek pleasure to numb it." Another miswiring might happen when you're a kid and have to run boring errands with your parents, like going to the bank, and then you get rewarded with a lollipop. "Bored? Seek pleasure to numb it."

Emotions = indicator lights

For the rest of the book, I'm going to use the term emotions to describe naturally occurring sensations and the term feelings as the meaning or label we assign to them. Most people aren't this literal, but it's important to differentiate between sensations in your body and the words we use because one of the most common glitchy files people create is "emotions = bad." When you're young, your emotions feel overwhelming and dangerous, or maybe you were told not to feel them ("Quit crying or I'll give you something to cry about!"), and so your brain makes a note: "emotions = bad." Since "emotions = bad" your brain stuffs them down, buries them, and any time an emotion threatens to come to the surface, you perceive a lack of safety. This leads to more fight/flight/freeze and more getting stuck with open loops.

The truth is emotions are better thought of as indicator lights. They're not good or bad. They're signals. And when you can allow them, you have an opportunity to check out the situation you're in and figure out what needs maintenance or attention. Instead of being a threat, your emotions are a request for a response. For instance, let's say you observe your heart racing and your palms sweating. You might have this filed as an indicator of danger. And it might be. Or it could be your body getting ready to perform. Either way, you can simply pause and notice, giving your prefrontal cortex a minute to catch up and formulate an appropriate response, rather than automatically packing more into that barrel by assuming the danger message is valid.

Once you reframe your emotions this way, you can start working actively with them instead of believing they happen to you. This will help you stay with yourself and create a sense of safety in your body, even when you're feeling "bad" or "scary" emotions –– which is key accessing and processing those old stuck loops.

Motivational style

Another thing that's helpful to know as you start the process of creating safety in your body is your motivational style. As we've discussed, most human brains function with the three survival goals of avoiding pain, seeking pleasure, and being efficient. However, we typically lean toward our stronger motivational style – we either run away from pain or run toward pleasure.

I run towards pleasure: I love to set goals. I imagine my future ideal state of being and use it to stay on track. My motivational style prefers running toward pleasure. When I began my health journey resulting in losing 30 pounds over six-months, I would say to myself, "A brownie won't taste as good as my ideal weight." For me, my ideal weight represented pleasure. As you begin the journey of calming your nervous systems by learning to allow your emotions, I think it's a good time to review your motivation style.

My husband primarily runs away from pain. One fall, he got on the scale and saw the highest number in his life, then the weather turned cold, and he struggled to button his jeans. He hated buying new jeans in THAT size, with a stretchy waistband. During his six-month health journey, he released 50 pounds. In the end, he bought jeans with smaller waistbands than he wore in high school with wiggle room.

You may be saying, "Angela, I don't like pain. I didn't want to feel my emotions the first time, so why would I want to do it afterward!" The fact of the matter remains, and science backs me up, if you don't deal with your emotions, they will eventually deal with you. According to Bessel van der Kolk, burying emotions can cause problems in the body, such as arthritis, joint or muscle pain, inflammation, diminished immunity, and a number of other diseases. The term psychosomatic is used when a medical issue is related to unresolved emotional issues. This doesn't mean it's in your head. It means it's buried emotions. Therefore, if you're motivated by avoiding pain, I hope you consider the long-term health impacts of not completing emotional cycles. Arthritis might not pop up right away, but it's an unpleasant future, for sure.

If you're motivated by moving toward pleasure, you may also be a bit apprehensive because completing the emotional cycles can be difficult, and it doesn't have the same outcome for everyone. For me, a portion of my weight loss came from dealing with some past unforgiveness and self-loathing. For one of my clients, she can now pitch her business with confidence and poise instead of terror and a squeaky voice. So, you go into this experience of learning to feel your emotions, not knowing what specific results await. The actual pleasure may be hard to identify at first, but it will emerge over time if you stick with it.

Window of tolerance

Finally, you need to know about the window of tolerance before you can start this process of calming your nervous system in preparation for completing your emotional loops. Developed by Dr. Dan Siegel, the window of tolerance describes the ideal emotional zone where you function optimally. It's between hyperarousal (which triggers fight or flight) or hypoarousal (which triggers freeze, numb, zoned out). When you are in the window of tolerance, you are calm, cool, collected, and connected. And you can increase your window of tolerance by soothing your nervous system, cleaning out your glitchy files, and processing those toxic waste barrels of negative beliefs. The wider it gets, the better you're able to manage your emotions and not be constantly hijacked by them.

So how do you increase your window of tolerance? By giving your brain new data to update those glitchy files. Let's take a basic example, like speaking in public even at a meeting in front of your colleagues. When you first start doing it, you may be scared and super activated (that's code for "Oh my gosh, I'm about to have a panic attack!"). When you can work through the fear, speak up, and see the consequences were not as bad as you thought, you slowly increase the window of tolerance. The more reps you get of not having the Earth open up and swallow you, the more your brain can calm down and re-file speaking in public as something safe or at least not dangerous.

The cool thing is your window of tolerance can always get bigger. I've been comfortable speaking in public for a long time. I've been in Toastmasters for 14 years! In 2015 I competed and won a Toastmasters District contest, which allowed me to attend the World Championship of Public Speaking. I loved speaking in front of an audience. It was my jam. I practiced for the contest by visiting other clubs, and I gave the same speech in front of other people a total of 13 different times. However, I was unprepared for the level of stage fright I would face when I went to Las Vegas and competed in my semi-final round. With a dry mouth, a racing heart, and a blank mind, I took the stage in front of 600 mostly empty chairs in a hotel ballroom. This was a new experience for me. I started competing in extemporaneous speech contests in high school and placed at State. I did pageants in high school, and I hung out with the Chancellor of the University of Arkansas as a campus leader my freshman year of college. I rarely felt stage fright until I got to the biggest stage of my life to that point. And you know what? I still did it. And my window of tolerance got even wider.

You can do the same thing with your window of tolerance, too –– and you'll get some great practice in opening it up when it comes to allowing your emotions.

Creating a sense of safety in your nervous system

When you first start to think about feeling your emotions, the whole concept can seem overwhelming and even dangerous. After all, if you start to feel one, another one opens up, and who knows what might happen? That's why it's key to create a sense of safety in your nervous system around this process. (Remember, if you don't feel safe and end up going into a stress response, you're just getting stuck in the same open loops.)

One way to think about this process is like you're taking a walk on the beach. It often seems like a good idea to stay away from the water, especially if there are big waves, it's cold, or you're wearing the wrong shoes. To compensate, you walk farther away from the water in the soft sand, and it's very hard going. Every step takes a lot of effort, like a fight with the sand. You don't get wet, but you tire out very quickly.

But if you walk closer to the water, you walk on the packed tight sand. It's not only easier to traverse, you don't get that soft sand stuck all over your feet. You can move faster. Occasionally a wave will come up and get your feet wet. But for the most part, enduring the waves is much easier than the safer part, where you have to fight against the sand with each step.

The prospect of resetting your nervous system and expressing your emotions can seem daunting like you'll be unprepared for the onslaught of waves. If you don't reset your nervous system, you'll end up choosing a smaller and smaller life to keep you safe – like trying to avoid the waves.

In actuality, as you begin to process past danger and pain, you resolve it so it doesn't continue to be an issue. You may still carry the scar of the pain, but it won't be scabbed over, ready to bleed at any moment. When you can go where it seems a bit more dangerous, you actually have a much easier time.

Methods for creating calm in your nervous system

Growth mindset

One of the hallmarks of toxic barrels is feeling "stuck" or like things just are the way they are, and there's nothing you can do about it. This is sometimes called a fixed mindset. One important first step to creating a sense of agency within yourself (which leads to more calm and safety within your nervous system) is adopting a growth mindset, as described by Carol Dweck. People with fixed mindsets believe their intelligence and talent are static and fixed. People with a growth mindset believe effort and learning can improve abilities, talent, and intelligence. Your invitation here is to adopt a growth mindset when it comes to your life and to this process. Just because you have a barrel with a big warning sign on it or a glitchy file telling you "the truth" about something doesn't mean you can't make a different decision.

Adopting a growth mindset may require additional effort, but the rewards are worth it. By embracing this mindset, we can design and shape our own lives according to our desires. Personally, I strive to believe that the life I currently have is the one I have consciously crafted. And I aim to silence the voice that suggests there may be greater possibilities if I were to embrace more success, failure, and impact. While circumstances may not always align with our plans, we gain control over our internal emotional well-being by cultivating a growth mindset and completing our emotional cycles, regardless of external events. This allows us to find contentment in the present and maintain hope for a better tomorrow.

Breathwork + body work

Breathing begins the physical process of creating safety in your body. After all, you can't take a deep breath and outrun a lion (or the neighbor's barking dog!) Deliberately deep breathing helps ground you in your body and tells your nervous system the message that things are OK, you are safe, and your prefrontal cortex can sound the all-clear. There are many methods of breathwork, but one way I do it is by imagining the breath as a fog, and I watch it float from my chest down to my diaphragm, into my stomach, and down to my pelvic bone. Each time I breathe in, I also imagine letting my muscles relax. When you stand, you can also imagine this breath flowing all the way to your toes. Watching your breath allows you to slow down and creates progressive relaxation.

Another method of getting in touch with your body and creating a sense of safety in your nervous system is the Feldenkrais® Method. I first experienced Feldenkrais® at a yoga studio. The gentle nature of the practice proves helpful and depends on very slight changes in movement. You can literally be sitting on the floor with your legs crossed and be told to move your knees toward the floor 1 degree. My instructor used it to recover from back surgery. When she started, she couldn't sit on the floor. She had to sit in a chair and begin to build movement up on her back, legs, and essentially her whole body. I think the first time I took the class, I chose it because of the convenient time, but I came to have a love/hate relationship with the practice. I found it incredibly frustrating. I disliked sitting still, and I sometimes couldn't make my body move 1 more degree because I wanted to move 10-15 degrees. My instructor offered the idea that how I felt in the class might represent something else in my life...like where else was I frustrated? Um, everywhere. (Clearly, she and my therapist were in league!)

Since then, I've come to see how it can help to really connect with your body. First, you tune into your bones. Your bones create the sturdiest part of you, essentially your foundation. Tap your heel, and sense the bones in your heel and your feet. Another helpful practice includes setting the intention of ease. "I have to decide to move with ease and to live with ease." Finally, you direct your attention to noticing everything happening in your body.

When you set the intention to feel your bones, you go beyond the muscles into deeper sensations, which then makes feeling the sensations in your muscles and identifying emotions a tiny bit easier. Sometimes when my clients get stuck while trying to feel the sensations in their bodies, I have them tap the heel of their foot on the ground and try to feel the bone while they do it. It has an incredible grounding effect. Even though these movements are small, being very gentle with your body is still important. If you've spent most of your life ignoring the warning signals from your nervous system, being gentle with yourself may be a completely new concept, and diving right in can be just as destructive as lifting too much weight too fast or running longer than your body has the capacity for.

A couple of other methods for connecting with your body and calming yourself: Dr. Peter Levine, the developer of Somatic Experiencing®, a naturalistic and neurobiological approach to healing trauma, has a few methods for regulating your body. One starts by putting your right hand over your heart. Try to feel your sternum, that bone that connects your ribs. Now put your left hand on your forehead. Notice your breathing. Leave your hands there until your breathing shifts and becomes more relaxed. When it changes, then move your left hand to your stomach. This technique is very calming. When you are in a meeting, you may look weird putting your hand on your forehead. If you have practiced in advance, you might try just resting your hand on your stomach and notice the warmth of your hand.

Another technique shared by Dr. Levine is to rub your hands down your arms, down your sides, and down your legs. You are literally trying to find the edges of your body so your body can contain the sensations you are experiencing. If you've ever sat and petted an animal for an extended period of time, you know this is very relaxing. This is similar, except you are kind of petting yourself.

The final technique, which I find helpful when I'm in a super-activated state is to notice my way through my five senses. What does that mean? Simply, if I'm in a meeting and it feels like my fight or flight system is coming online, I can tune in to what I see, what I smell, what I can hear, what is touching my body, and what I taste in my mouth. Ever tasted the iron-like flavor of fear in your mouth? It's weird and hard to admit to.

Hopefully, these techniques will begin to build new coping skills to allow your nervous system to complete emotional cycles at the moment and when you begin processing the toxic waste. I've found that by learning new coping mechanisms to calm myself down, wading into the water of incomplete emotions seems less daunting.

Imagination

Now let's shift from your body to your mind and talk about the importance of imagination in the process. Did you know when your brain imagines something, your subconscious doesn't know what's real and what's made up? Olympic athletes use their imagination to visualize completing their routine flawlessly, and extensive research studies have proven this an effective tool for improvement. One study had a group of people physically practice free throws, vs. another group only mentally practiced the free throws. The people who physically practiced improved by 24%, and those who practiced in their imagination improved by 23%.

Visualization is an incredibly effective practice for nurturing imagination and creativity. My journey with visualization began when I was pregnant with Sami. During a Lamaze class, our instructor encouraged us to envision our happy place. I closed my eyes and pictured a serene meadow, exploring its beauty until I stumbled upon a breathtaking rose bush. Dr. Ruth Lanius, the esteemed Director of the PTSD research unit at the University of Western Ontario, would describe this as a sacred space—a refuge in our minds, free from intrusion, threat, and pain.

Years later, I employed this technique to deepen my relationship with God. With closed eyes, I asked Him to reveal a place where I could always connect with Him. Initially, it was a cozy living room adorned with captivating artwork, cool couches, and a comforting fireplace. This became my go-to place to commune with God in my mind's eye. I familiarized myself with every nook and cranny, taking the time to explore and soak in its atmosphere. I would then imagine sitting on the couch, engaging in heartfelt conversations with Jesus about all aspects of my life. Often, I found myself doing this during the worship sessions at church, feeling an incredible sense of worship and closeness to God. The book The Shack expanded my understanding, offering new perspectives on how to experience the presence of God in this imagined realm.

The final way to nurture your imagination is by incorporating a safe attachment figure. Picture someone in your life who has always loved you unconditionally, provided unwavering support, and had your best interests at heart. This person serves as your safe attachment figure, and they can play a vital role in boosting your imagination. Whenever you find yourself faced with a decision about how you want to feel regarding a certain situation, your safe attachment figure can offer you invaluable wisdom and guidance. They become a trusted advisor, helping you navigate your emotions and choose the best path forward.

Additionally, this safe attachment figure is crucial for your healing journey. It could be a beloved pet, a special person in your life (like a grandparent), or even a higher power you believe in. The key is to have someone you can imagine talking to at any time, especially when you're learning to quiet your mind and work through emotional challenges.

By visualizing conversations with your safe attachment figure, you can find solace, gain insights, and achieve a sense of completion for unresolved emotions. They provide a comforting presence and serve as a valuable resource as you cultivate your imagination and foster emotional well-being.

Curiosity and compassion

This whole process only works with curiosity and compassion. Curiosity is a strong desire to know or learn something. Compassion is to recognize the distress of others with a desire to relieve that distress. Curiosity requires psychological safety. So, if you are afraid, you will be attacked -- even by yourself! -- for having the wrong answer, you will keep quiet instead of being openly curious. Your psychological safety begins with you. Do you have your own back? When you make a mistake, does the critical voice beat you up and make you more rigid?

When you notice you are doing something you've said time and again you don't want to do, instead of beating yourself up, access your compassion. Then try the phrase: "Of course, that makes sense." As we talked about in earlier chapters, your brain is trying to reconcile what happened and make sense of it. When we affirm to ourselves that what we are thinking or experiencing makes sense, it creates safety. When you've been in a negative thought pattern for a long time, of course, it makes sense that it would be hard to change. When learning a new skill, it often takes many reps to get it right. Of course, it makes sense that you make mistakes.

Using this gentleness with yourself promotes safety, allows you to feel your emotions, and cultivates a deeper love which, in turn, you can show others. At the end of the day, your body is desperate to know the answer to the question: Do you have your own back? The whole world is full of people who may criticize you (probably because of their own self-judgment and self-loathing), and you have to quit that team and be a better coach to yourself. As you continue this journey, you will develop your own emotional regulation toolbox.

Fellow travelers

Likewise, addressing personal issues in a group setting with fellow travelers can be advantageous. Whether you choose to join a mastermind group, engage with Celebrate Recovery, Alcoholics Anonymous, or explore other options tailored to your needs, the benefits of sharing your journey with others are numerous and diverse. Not only can you gain valuable insights from others on how to process emotions, but you can also find solace in the fact that you're not alone in unpacking your personal challenges.

If you encounter areas where you notice resistance to delve deeper, having a trusted group of truth-tellers can also provide the necessary support and accountability. This group can offer you guidance, knowledge, and understanding, helping you navigate through your personal growth journey. By holding you accountable for your actions and encouraging you to confront difficult emotions or patterns, they create a safe space for you to address and overcome obstacles, promoting your overall well-being and growth.

Everything starts with a decision

Do you remember how your inner strength and resilience have always influenced your mental and emotional well-being? Just as when you face the challenge of riding uphill or tackling a difficult problem, your initial frustration can make the task seem insurmountable. However, when you approach it from a positive and empowered mindset, you'll find that the obstacles that tripped you up yesterday have become much easier to overcome.

This same principle holds true for your current situation. We are now embarking on a journey to explore and acknowledge your emotions, and this process requires a conscious decision from you. What will you decide? Will you summon the determination to face the uphill battle head-on, or will you allow doubt and uncertainty to hold you back? Remember, the choice is yours, and it is through this choice that you will pave the way toward emotional growth and healing.

To sum up:

It is important to understand the distinctions between emotions and feelings and recognize your unique motivational style and capacity to tolerate different emotional states to embark on the emotional healing journey. This understanding serves as the initial step in rewiring any faulty patterns that may exist within you.

As we delve into the process of addressing unresolved emotions, it will be crucial for you to equip yourself with healthy coping mechanisms that can soothe your nervous system. These tools will play a significant role as we navigate through the complexities of untangling emotional knots.

In the beginning, it's natural to feel overwhelmed. However, you can remain connected to compassion and curiosity by employing various breathing techniques, creating a safe mental space, and envisioning a trusted figure for support. These resources will be invaluable as you embark on this transformative journey.

CHAPTER 6
Completing the cycles

Your toolbox of emotional regulation just got some major upgrades. For starters, knowledge is power. Recognizing the difference between how we are naturally wired for survival versus how our experiences create incorrect programming helps to encourage us that if a information gets misfiled, it can be changed. Second, by understanding how the filing system works, you can decide as an adult how you want the filing to be. Finally, by learning how to begin to regulate your nervous system, you will begin to see how you are truly in the driver's seat of your life. You've gone so much further into an understanding of yourself than most people ever will. Now it's time to get into the meat of the work: processing emotions so you can clear out those toxic barrels once and for all!

This sounds simple on the surface. But the truth is, no one outside of therapy teaches us how to feel our emotions. We think it's a verbal exercise. And while our conscious mind does play a part later in the process, that's not the full extent of experiencing your emotions. Similarly, you might think you need to talk about your emotions in a specific way to feel them. "This thing happened; here's how I felt."

Again, that can be important, but that comes later in the process. It took me a while to get this -- as a positive-thinking evangelist, I used to believe that if I felt something unpleasant, I just needed to think a new thought. But then I learned there's a step before choosing the new thought: experiencing the emotions first.

As we talked about previously, emotions and feelings are all different. Emotions are real-time data sparked by sensations in the body. Feelings can be more biased and altered by mental misconceptions. When things happened that didn't feel safe to feel at the time, you buried the incomplete emotional cycles in these metaphorical barrels. If you're trying to process one of those belief barrels, it's not enough to change the belief cognitively. You have to complete the emotional cycle to remove the charge. And that's what we're about to get into.

Discovering incomplete cycles

I say that on a day-to-day basis, most people can deal with their life and the sensations generated. However, when outside our comfort zone, such as trying to reach a new goal or tackling a new challenge, we are triggered, and our barrels explode and make a mess. By controlling the blast, we can clear the field systematically.

When it comes to knowing where to begin, let me share a metaphor that I find quite fitting: gardening. Imagine your life as a garden, a fertile ground that yields various fruits such as relationships, goal achievement, and emotional well-being.

Typically we become willing to change only when the pain of staying the same is too great. So, take a moment to check out your life's garden. Are you happy with the fruits it produces? Do you find genuine satisfaction in your relationships with others, your approach to food and nourishment, your relationship with alcohol, and your choice of leisure activities? If any of these areas leave you unsatisfied, it could indicate something is amiss within your garden, and you have some emotional cycles to clear.

Dr. Peter Levine says the posture we hold could be another indicator of an incomplete emotional cycle. We have different types of memory. One is procedural memory: like driving a car or brushing your teeth. If you have spent your childhood flinching because you were afraid you would be hit or scrunching smaller because you didn't want to draw attention to yourself, you could have a posture that shows you that you have an incomplete emotional cycle around this.

Another indicator of where to start is if you have unexplained pain or a recurring illness. I have several clients that have had excellent success noticing patterns of unexplained pain by creating a detailed timeline of their life. (Think: major events like birth, deaths, marriage, divorce, job or address changes, health history, and significant achievements or disappointments.) Sometimes this timeline reveals you had major pain, trauma, or disappointment in your life that you thought you dealt with, then two years later, you had an unexplained issue with your body, perhaps your heart. Without a written account of the items in your life, you may not see the connection between the two because of the time-lapse.

It's worth covering again. Sometimes when we talk about the pain rooted in emotion, people hear, "Oh, you think it's all in your head." Nope. As I mentioned previously about arthritis, if we have emotional pain that we don't have the skills to deal with or we refuse to acknowledge, our body will try to get our attention. Over time it won't just try. It absolutely will get your attention. However, most of us treat pain and illness as something we need medicine for and don't realize this is also an indicator light, so we don't realize we are supposed to explore the pain for emotional issues that haven't been resolved.

Some examples of common psychosomatic symptoms are:
- Fatigue
- Insomnia
- Aches and pains, such as muscle pain or back pain
- High blood pressure (hypertension)
- Trouble breathing (dyspnea or shortness of breath)
- Indigestion (upset stomach)
- Headaches and migraines

One of the most impactful experiences I had regarding psychosomatic pain occurred during my time spent with my dear friend, Theresa. She was enduring excruciating back pain that hindered her ability to walk to the mailbox. She tried wearing a brace, using a cane, and nothing really helped. Theresa and I were both patients of the same chiropractor, and our oldest children were close friends. One day, she confided in me that her neurosurgeon had informed her that the only potential solution for relief was to undergo spinal fusion surgery, fusing two vertebrae together with a metal plate. The doctor believed that the pain stemmed from the movement of the vertebrae rubbing against each other. Although the surgery would enable her to walk again, there was no guarantee it would eliminate the pain. As with any surgery, there were also risks involved that were very scary for her.

Having witnessed remarkable healing through attending prayer sessions at our church's prayer room, where emotional issues often surfaced alongside physical ailments, I encouraged Theresa to give it a try. However, she approached the idea with skepticism. Determined to convince her, I pleaded, "Theresa, you're on the verge of undergoing life-altering spinal surgery. I'm willing to sacrifice a few hours on a Sunday night to see if this could provide any help. The worst-case scenario is a couple of hours spent praying."

During the prayer session, Theresa was instructed to seek guidance from God about the cause of her pain. Suddenly, tears streamed down her face, and she shared a deeply buried secret—her husband had tragically lost his life in the 1983 bombing of the Marine barracks in Beirut. Theresa had erected an emotional wall around the incident, not discussing it, rarely sharing the story even with her current husband. In a striking parallel, the surgeon's proposed physical fusion mirrored the emotional barrier she had constructed within herself.

I cannot claim that she experienced an immediate and complete recovery, but she did feel an immediate alleviation of the pain's intensity. Fast forward more than ten years, and

Theresa never underwent the surgery. She now walks 3-4 times a week for at least 3-4 miles and frequently bikes as well. She has continued her journey of healing, and when she visits the neurosurgeon twice a year, he marvels at her progress, she calls herself a walking miracle. Despite her MRI remaining unchanged, her pain has vanished, eliminating the need for surgery.

Psychosomatic pain is an extensive topic, far beyond this book. However, it is important to recognize that when you encounter unexplained pain or recurring illnesses, especially if you hear the discouraging phrase, "The doctors don't know what's wrong with me," it is likely rooted in emotions that demand acknowledgment and processing.

If no obvious physical signs like posture or physical pain indicate an incomplete cycle, you can rely on your imagination to identify incomplete cycles. This approach is highly effective for me and provides me with significant control over the situation. When something happens that activates me, I usually need my emotions to settle down quickly so that I can finish what I'm doing or the conversation I'm having. Through the use of my imagination, I can place myself in situations that have triggered responses in the past and give myself the space to process the emotions in a safe environment. For instance, I might envision setting a challenging goal, engaging in a difficult conversation, or making a major life change. By creating these scenarios within the realm of imagination, I can explore the associated emotions and show my brain how to navigate and survive the sensations. A major focus of my coaching work revolves around facilitating this type of emotional completion. I thoroughly enjoy helping people who feel stuck in various areas of their lives by uncovering the incomplete emotional cycles that contribute to their stuckness or inability to achieve their goals.

In the final technique, I guide clients through an exercise that involves reflecting on something they have great confidence in, such as their role as a parent, friend, or business person. I then go through each of those seven common beliefs we talked about earlier and ask them to rate, on a scale of one to ten, how true they believe each belief is. For example, when considering their ability to be a good friend, I ask them to assess the extent to which they feel they are enough. I record the scores for each of the seven beliefs. Next, I have them think about an area where they lack confidence or struggle, such as being a parent, friend, or business person. Again, I ask them to assign a numeric score between one and ten to indicate how true they believe each belief is. For instance, when contemplating their capability as a business owner, I inquire about the truth of the statement "I am enough."

Then, I compare the scores for each belief between the area of confidence and the area of struggle. For instance:
• As a friend, the belief "I am enough" scored a 8.
• As a mom, the belief "I am enough" scored a 5.

Ultimately, we address and resolve all the beliefs using a process I will explain shortly. However, we begin with the belief that exhibits the greatest disparity between the two areas (confidence and struggle), as this approach has proven to be highly effective.

Creating safety

Once you know what loops you're going to work on closing, the first goal is to stabilize your nervous system. (Said another way, you want to feel safe in your body.) This is key because until you're able to create a place of safety, you won't be able to notice or fully process the outstanding emotions. You've done a lot of work towards being more at home in your nervous system, generally in the last chapter, but it's important that you take the time to create a sense of safety at the beginning of each loop-closing session.

So, how do you create safety? By beginning to make space for your body and heart to be honest about what's really happening. Sometimes I talk with people who have a lot of negative self-talk, things like,

"Suck it up, buttercup."

Or,

"Other people have it so much worse than I do. What is my problem?"

I ask them if they have a niece or nephew that is 10 to 13 years old. This seems more applicable than even a child because, with our children, we sometimes make their actions mean something about our parenting. As an aunt or uncle, the secondary nature of the relationship allows a different type of trust and communication. When I ask if they would say these negative things to their niece or nephew, they respond with either an appalled "Of course not" or a sheepish "No." Either way, when you say those things to yourself, you say those things to the 10 or 12 –year old version of yourself in your mind. Your inner child longs for unconditional love, not the contempt you spew.

Most people who consider learning to finish incomplete cycles related to their childhood may possibly give some haughty answer like, "That doesn't affect me anymore. I'm over it." If you believe this way now, I really hope your brain begins to notice the ways that you could start to release your emotions in a healthy way, and you can be a bit gentler with yourself. As you begin to notice what's happening in your body, I hope it gives you the confidence to start talking about it. And your identity changes into someone ready to allow their emotions and complete their emotional cycles.

Some people can create safety and subsequently release their emotions in meditation, but I had to start with physical activity. It seemed like I had to give my nervous system something else to focus on to allow myself to quiet the mind chatter. I also used this time to talk to God, a very recentering practice for me. When you begin to notice your emotions, it will feel like getting to know yourself in a different way. Don't be afraid to incorporate walking, running, biking, walking your dog, or some physical exercise while you get reacquainted with what it's actually like inside your body. Studies indicate during physical exercise, especially endurance activities like running or biking, your body shifts to autopilot to allow your brain to wander. Dr. Megan Cannon, a sport psychologist, suggests your brain receives permission to let go as your body gets tired. This allows us to relax our guard and let the emotions flow.

The most important thing here is to find a way that you can feel safe and still involved with what you're experiencing. It may be very tempting to distract yourself, especially at first, but stick with it. Stay focused on the end goal of eliminating the pain that plagues you (nagging negative thoughts) or the pleasure you hope to achieve (peaceful thoughts). If you keep distracting yourself, you will allow your life to slip by without any intentional effort.

Finally, avoid mistaking resistance for lack of safety. Dr. Steven Hayes, the founder of Acceptance and Commitment Therapy, says to expect resistance because becoming more conscious takes a lot of effort, and our brain prefers to avoid hard things by nature. Self-kindness and self-compassion assist the journey far more than judgment and ridicule.

Noticing sensations

Once you've created that setting of safety, it's time to start noticing your emotions. A helpful technique is called a body scan. I often ask my new clients to imagine going through an MRI scan of their body. They begin at their toes and slowly scan each part of their body, all the way up to the top of their head. The goal is to notice any areas that feel tense or uneasy. When they reach their head, I ask them to go back to their shoulders, as that's a common area for holding tension. You've probably heard the phrase "carrying the weight of the world on your shoulders" –– well, it's not just a saying. Our stress tends to accumulate there, especially if we spend a lot of time hunched over computers and cell phones. While it may not seem directly related to emotions, think about it: do those devices bring you good news, peace, and joy all day? I didn't think so.

I then guide my clients to notice and describe the sensations of tension in their shoulders. It's a safe area to explore because it's quite common. Surprisingly, just by becoming aware of the sensations, they often experience a change and release of tension in their neck. After practicing with something safe like neck tension, we move on to working through the belief list from the previous chapter. For example, I ask them to think the thought "I am enough" and pay attention to the sensations that show up in their body.

The most important step here is to slow down. If you're in fight or flight, your breathing gets shallow, and your mind begins to race or go into hyper-slow motion. Slowing your body's natural response by pausing and taking a deep breath is a good idea. This one very small action begins sending the signal to your brain that the threat you're perceiving isn't as dire as you initially thought. Next, notice in your body where you are feeling the stress. When you think the thought, I am enough, did your stomach clench? Heart race? Shoulders get tight? Really think about where you are noticing sensations. This action continues to communicate to your brain that the threat is not dire. Now describe the way your body is reacting further. Is it hot, cold, or warm? Is it a shooting sensation, gripping, or tightening? Is there a color associated with it? What shape is it? Does it seem like a swirling circle or a swirling ball? You want to get very granular. What is the texture? Flat, round, jagged? Focus on the sensation. When you focus on it, does it change? Does it get worse?

Once you've started to get a handle on what sensations you are experiencing, just continue to notice the sensation and sit with it, watching it grow, change or shrink. You aren't trying to get rid of the feeling. You are practicing allowing it. If possible, be grateful for the sensation. It's here to give you information, so even if it's unpleasant, it's for your benefit. Gratitude for something unpleasant is extremely difficult.

I encourage clients to walk around the sensation as if they are at a museum studying an exhibit they are very interested in. Zoom in. Zoom out. Walk all around. As you sit with this reaction/sensation, it will begin to change. It may grow in intensity, spread, or settle in to stay the same. As long as it keeps changing, just describe it again. The shape got bigger or smaller; swirling is more intense, less intense. Sometimes people want to label it and say something like I feel sadness. I encourage them that we aren't interested in labeling it right now. We are simply describing the sensations. Try not to even label something as pain. It's just a sensation. Pain is actually a label. I have cheated on this and called it unpleasant, but do as I say, not as I do. If your stomach feels like it's swirling, notice how large the swirling sensation is.

Notice how it continues to change or shift places. Notice the temperature and color changes. Does it get more intense or less intense? You are becoming a noticer and a describer of what's happening in your body. This may feel unnatural at first. It may also seem like you are making up a color or a shape. At least, that's what my clients tell me when I'm leading them through it. They often wonder if they are just saying words because I asked them to. I try to offer shapes, colors, and descriptions of tension. I also encourage them that there may not be a shape, color, or noticeable tension, and that's OK. We are just noticing. Eventually, the sensation may dissipate. If it does, it may be that your body just needed you to pay attention.

If it settles into one place and stops moving around, it may be ready to give you the message it's been trying to get you to notice.

Once you've gotten to that point, ask the sensation what it has to tell you. It sounds super woo-woo but it is actually incredibly important. It may feel weird when you ask the sensation what it wants to tell you. I encourage clients to imagine they are handing a microphone to the shape they've been describing then just be really quiet. Typically your brain will deliver the message in a few different ways. It could be a word, phrase, picture, or video that may seem to play in your mind, or a random story may pop into your memory, like my friend Theresa who suddenly remembered the story of her husband dying 30 years previously. One client had the phrase pop into their mind, "You don't have to keep score anymore." I asked her if that meant something to her. She said yes. She felt like she was always working against a scorecard in her head to prove she was enough.

Sometimes even if an emotion settles into one place, it doesn't seem to have a message. If this happens, it can be helpful to dial things up. This can help make the emotion more noticeable and help you process it faster. The way you do this is to imagine the worst case you can of whatever the perceived threat is. If you are still working with the thought I am enough, imagine a scenario where you felt like you were definitely NOT enough. How does the reaction change? Can you amp up the reaction to 100?

Warning: this can be extremely unpleasant. And you're not actually in danger. You know when your feet are so cold that they've gone numb, and when the feeling comes back, it's like knives being stabbed in your feet? Even though you're not actually being stabbed with knives, it feels so horrible. And you will survive.

After amplifying the sensation, simply allow it to run its course. The objective at this stage is not to eliminate the sensation, but rather to let it complete its cycle.

Once the sensation delivers its message, it might completely fade away or significantly diminish. Occasionally, it may intensify momentarily to emphasize its point before eventually dissipating.

While it may temporarily grow in intensity, if you stay present with the sensation, it will eventually start to diminish and likely disappear. You might find that shedding tears helps to alleviate it, or engaging in physical movements such as squirming, jumping jacks, or moving your head and feet from side to side. Remember the instance when I had to pause grief processing to go for a run. Trust your body's instincts.

If the sensation persists, it could be because your body still doubts that you will pay attention to the message. This is more common with clients who experience tingling sensations in their hands or arms. It's as if your body wants to leave a lingering reminder of this new understanding until you fully embrace it.

Allowing emotions

So much of this work is allowing unpleasant emotions and sensations -- and you may find yourself resisting this. It was a bit hard to comprehend when I first became aware of this. Why would I allow unpleasant feelings if my thoughts create my feelings? You might be avoidant too, fighting the sensation on and on and on because you don't want to feel bad. But that's like trying to hold the beach ball under the water. If you pause and lean into the sensations and reactions in your body, you can remove resistance and move pretty quickly through the sensations, at least the acute ones.

What I'm learning is that when you decide to allow your emotions at the moment, it doesn't take that long. One day, I got super triggered because I was working in a direct sales organization as a health coach. The next rank that I was working toward was executive director. I was on a training conference call, and I started bawling. I mean ugly crying because this was a month after I got fired from being the executive director at the housing authority. I had enough sense and trust in Barry that I went down to his office, and he hugged me while I cried. The whole process took maybe 10-15 minutes from the first trigger until I quit crying. I was still able to complete the training, just sniffing and wiping my eyes. It didn't ruin my day. An hour later, I was sitting at lunch with a friend and potential client who was just pouring out his heart about his dream. We agreed to the terms of the agreement to work together on a super fun project. Crying out the emotions that came up didn't take very long, and then I could be emotionally free for the rest of the day. I didn't have the metaphorical beach ball waiting to smack me in the face when I was least expecting it.

What I've learned throughout this process is to be fully human, fully evolved, and fully alive is to feel the whole range of emotions. When we limit ourselves to only allow positive emotions, we limit those positive emotions. A tall mountain is characterized by a deep valley. In the same way, the willingness to feel the depths of sadness when we lose someone really important to us allows us to reach heights of staggering joy.

That's why it is important to be aware of ways you might unintentionally hinder or avoid this emotional processing. Two common examples of this are lashing out and distracting yourself. Throughout this book, we have discussed the significance of incomplete emotional cycles, which occur when we don't allow emotions to naturally run their course.

However, expressing negative feelings in a hurtful manner towards others does not complete the cycle; instead, it turns you into a tornado of emotions. Acknowledging and accepting that you are experiencing emotions is crucial to complete the cycle. Allow the wave of sensations to flow through its natural rhythm. Take the time to understand what triggered these sensations and why you are feeling the way you do. Listen to the message these emotions are conveying. If necessary, identify the cause of the activation before releasing it and moving forward. By following these steps, you can effectively complete the emotional cycle at the moment and continue on your journey of growth and healing.

Alternatively, old habits might kick in, and you automatically try to numb your feelings by eating, drinking, or binging on a screen. I discovered when I'm bored, I seem to develop an insatiable hunger. Also, if I'm at a party where I don't feel like I can be myself, I find myself hovering at the food table to have someone (the food) keep me company. Brooke Castillo, founder of The Life Coach School, where I got my life coach certification, explains if we can't tolerate boredom, it's a reflection of how much we are willing to spend time with ourselves. If we can be curious about our brains, then there's an endless amount of stuff to alleviate boredom. Additionally, she says if you want to accomplish great things, it is wise to cultivate boredom. How many great ideas have you had in the shower? It's because your brain has space to wander. When you're constantly consuming --food, alcohol, or media -- you don't have any capacity left for thinking deeper thoughts, solving harder problems, or dreaming bigger dreams. Consuming reduces your creativity.

Each emotion you feel has a purpose and can aid in your ability to respond. Emotions are typically meant to protect us (avoid pain) or connect us (increase pleasure). When you feel the sensation at the moment, you then get to decide what it means. This is why it's true that your thoughts create your feelings because when you decide what it means, you are labeling a feeling. When you notice the sensation, you are simply experiencing an emotion. A friend told me that her husband said, "When I go on a roller coaster, my stomach does flips, my heart is racing, and I feel dizzy." She replied, "I know, isn't it great?" He was shocked to find that she felt the exact same thing, but for her, she went on the roller coaster because she liked the flipping dizziness.

When deciding what the sensations in your body mean, you may run across many random thoughts. Sometimes you don't have to make them mean anything. Have you ever been out in a boat on the lake? When you see another boat, what do you do? You wave as you continue on your way. You don't stop the boat and ask them over for tea. You just wave. Sometimes our thoughts resemble the passing boat. You can just wave at it as it goes on by. If you get distracted while noticing the sensations in your body sitting with yourself, wave at the boat and start again.

To sum up:

In this chapter, we explored the concept of discovering incomplete cycles as a means to identify areas where emotional processing is needed. By using our imagination, we can create a safe environment to explore and process these emotions, even in the absence of physical signs. Creating a sense of safety is crucial in this process, allowing us to tune into our emotions without fear or judgment.

We discussed the technique of a body scan, where we systematically scan our bodies from toes to head, identifying areas of tension or unease. Noticing these sensations and acknowledging them is a key step in emotional healing. By allowing ourselves to experience and describe these sensations, we can begin to release the built-up tension and experience a sense of relief.

In the next chapter, we'll delve into the transformative power of replacing toxic barrels with helpful positive beliefs. By embracing new skills and perspectives, we can move from a survival mindset to a thriving one, empowering us to pursue and achieve our dreams.

CHAPTER 7
Planting new beliefs

The progress you have made is freaking awesome. (You didn't think I'd go the whole book without using my catchphrase, did you?) You have taken courageous steps to explore the inner workings of your mind and emotions. You have begun the essential task of processing your emotions and transforming the toxic waste that resides within you into a safe and nurturing space.

So, as we embark on this chapter dedicated to planting new beliefs, let us pause and celebrate your accomplishments. I am truly proud of the strides you have taken and the resilience you have shown. I encourage you to take a moment to acknowledge your own strength and courage. You have come a long way, and your progress deserves recognition.

How can you celebrate? Give yourself a high five? Send me a message on Instagram? Do a little happy dance? Even take a deep breath. I'm so proud of you and hope you are proud of yourself.

The work's not done yet, though. As you complete these cycles and feel your emotions, you're going to want to start replacing those old beliefs with something new. Think about it like environmental rehabilitation. We've dug out the toxic waste and landmines. Now the land is safe for use. So I invite you to put some intentionality behind it and deliberately plant some seeds that will grow into new, healthy beliefs that serve you. This will not only support your life, but also keep weeds (AKA remnants of old beliefs) from popping back up.

Planting new beliefs

While you probably didn't have a lot of conscious control over the beliefs that made up your toxic waste barrels, you now get to decide what new beliefs you want to plant. Remember the seven core beliefs I had categorized as unhelpful in my life? I found it very helpful to turn those beliefs around, replacing them with a positive form. Now I'm inviting you to do this too. You might have some of the same beliefs, or yours might differ. Either way, try to get a strong understanding of what each of them means and how you can apply them. This gives them healthy roots –– think of it as adding fertilizer to the garden of your life.

Let's walk through the seven beliefs I talked about to get us started:
- I am lovable
- I am enough
- I belong
- I am valuable
- I am worthy
- I trust myself
- I have what it takes

I am lovable

Synonyms: precious, endearing

Since the definition of lovable is inspiring or deserving of love or having qualities that make a person easy to love, I think it would also be helpful to define love. Love is an unselfish, loyal, and benevolent concern for the good of another; cherish; actively desire, or take pleasure in.

The English language significantly lacks the nuance of love. Let's look to the Greek language since they have eight different words for love.

Eros – physical love or sexual desire; involves passion, lust and/or romance.

Philia – affectionate love; deep friendship. (Philadelphia is known as the City of Brotherly Love.)

Agape – unconditional, sacrificial love; willingness to do anything for another without expecting anything in return.

Storge – familial love; the natural affection family members have for one another. This protective type of love typically feels safe and cared for, not passionate. It could also describe team sports and country allegiance.

Mania – obsessive love, like that of a stalker. i.e., pyromania, a stalker type of love of fire.

Erotoropia or ludus – playful, flirtatious, noncommittal love. Ludus means game or play, which describes this type of love.

Pragma – practical love based in duty, obligation, or logic. While eros is fun, pragma is enduring. It makes an effort to give, not just receive.

Philautia – self-love, in how a person views themselves and how they feel about their own body. Aristotle said, "All friendly feelings for others are an extension of a man's feelings for himself."

Being lovable is a fundamental truth that exists irrespective of conditions or accomplishments. Dr. Sue Johnson, creator of Emotionally Focused Therapy, explains in her book *Love Sense* that love is necessary to our survival more than ever before in human history. It is not contingent on ticking off items from your to-do list or constantly pleasing others. Simply by virtue of being alive, you are lovable. You deserve love and affection, not because of anything you do, but because you exist. Embracing this belief is about recognizing your inherent worthiness of love and accepting it into your life. You are lovable, just as you are.

Consider the love given to a newborn baby. They are not expected to earn love or meet certain criteria; it is freely and unconditionally bestowed upon them. The same applies to you. You are deserving of love simply by being who you are. This teaching is echoed by Jesus, and many other faiths affirm that we are to love our neighbor as ourselves. By cultivating self-love, you align yourself with the golden rule of treating others with love and compassion.

Recognizing your own lovability does not diminish anyone else's worthiness of love. On the contrary, the more you love and accept yourself, the easier it becomes to love and accept others. Self-love serves as the bedrock for all your relationships. When you believe in your own lovability, it becomes natural to receive and appreciate the love that others offer rather than dismissing it or questioning their judgment. By embracing your own lovability, you create a positive ripple effect that enhances your connections with others.

Remember, loving yourself does not make you selfish or egocentric. It is a transformative act of self-care and acceptance that allows you to show up authentically and offer genuine love to others. Embrace the truth that you are lovable without the need for external validation or conditions. Embodying this belief empowers you to experience deeper connections, foster healthier relationships, and live a more fulfilling life. You are lovable, and it's time to fully embrace and celebrate that truth.

I belong

Synonyms: be part of, fit, exist, associate, be linked with

Belonging means to be in the right place; to feel happy or comfortable in a situation; to be suitable; appropriate, or advantageous; bound by birth, allegiance, or dependency; have proper qualifications, especially social qualifications; a member of a group.

Belonging starts with yourself. I belong. It is an essential aspect of human existence, rooted in our innate desire for interpersonal connections and social bonds. Extensive research has confirmed that the need to belong is a fundamental motivation that drives our behaviors and shapes our well-being. It is a universal human need, deeply ingrained in our sense of identity and purpose. While the degree of belongingness may vary from person to person, the longing to feel accepted and connected is inherent in all of us.

When we belong, we experience a sense of belonging, which brings us comfort, support, and a shared sense of identity. Belonging provides a framework for avoiding pain and seeking pleasure, as we find solace in being part of a group or community. However, it's important to note that true belonging starts from within. It begins with accepting and embracing yourself, feeling comfortable in your own skin, and cultivating a deep connection with your own values, beliefs, and aspirations.

Belonging to yourself means recognizing that you are a unique and valuable individual worthy of love, acceptance, and belonging. It is about finding your place in the world, honoring your authentic self, and celebrating the qualities that make you who you are. When you have a strong sense of belonging to yourself, you can navigate any situation, even in a crowded room, with a deep sense of self-assuredness and inner alignment. By affirming "I belong," you acknowledge your rightful place in the world and assert your intrinsic worthiness.

Remember that belonging is not about conforming to societal expectations or seeking validation from others. It is about fostering a deep sense of self-acceptance, self-compassion, and self-love. By nurturing your own belongingness, you create a solid foundation for connecting with others authentically and building meaningful relationships. Embrace the truth that you belong, both to yourself and to the world, and allow this positive belief to shape your experiences, interactions, and overall sense of fulfillment.

I am enough

Synonyms: adequate, satisfactory, sufficient, suitable, competent

Enough means as much as required; a sufficient amount; occurring in such quantity, quality, or scope to fully meet demands, needs, or expectations.

The concept of "enough" encompasses having an ample and satisfactory quantity, quality, or scope that fully meets demands, needs, or expectations. When you hold the belief that you are enough, it means recognizing that you possess a sufficient amount to fulfill your wants or needs and are capable of satisfying your desires. It's essential to understand that your past does not define you; it is a part of your journey but not the entirety of who you are. While you may have made mistakes, separating those actions from your intrinsic worth is crucial. You are not defined by your mistakes; you are not mistakes yourself. You are enough.

By acknowledging that comparison and seeking external validation do not determine your true essence, you can let go of the belief that you are not enough and instead embrace self-acceptance and self-love. It is through embracing your individual strengths and setting healthy boundaries that you can liberate yourself from the constraints of this belief. In this process, you can nurture a sense of empowerment and fulfillment by acknowledging your inherent qualities and living in alignment with your own values rather than being dictated by the expectations of others.

Recognizing that you are enough empowers you to take control of your self-perception. You determine how you think of yourself and refuse to let others dictate your view of yourself. Self-acceptance stems from the belief that you are enough just as you are. Even if you want to continue evolving, you are enough as you are right now. This is not an invitation for mediocrity. It's living to your standards. Embracing this belief enables you to embrace your true self without the need for external validation or comparison. You acknowledge your strengths, unique qualities, and the value you bring to the world. You are enough, and this affirmation resonates within you, shaping your self-image and fostering a sense of wholeness and contentment.

I am valuable

Synonyms: priceless, premium, extravagant, treasured, relevant, worthwhile, prized, important, beneficial, helpful

`Valuable means very helpful; important; useful; beneficial; having desirable or esteemed characteristics or qualities; of considerable service.

Understanding and embracing your own value is paramount in shaping your life. Being valuable means more than just being helpful, important, or useful. It encompasses possessing desirable qualities and esteemed characteristics that contribute significantly to the world around you. When something loses its value, it becomes dispensable, easily discarded. In the same way, feeling valuable acts as a protective shield against the fear of being cast aside or overlooked. When you truly value yourself, it creates a powerful barrier that deflects the negative comments and opinions of others.

You are valuable, and recognizing this belief allows you to accept your strengths and determine areas where you want to continue to increase that value to yourself. By investing in yourself, prioritizing your well-being, pursuing your dreams, and setting boundaries that honor your heart and its desires, you can plant this belief deep in your mind. Remember, you are deserving of love, respect, and a fulfilling life, regardless of any external circumstances or past experiences.

So, I want you to remember this: You are valuable. Embrace and celebrate your value, for it is the essence of who you are. As you recognize yourself as a treasure to be cared for, you pave the way for a life filled with self-acceptance, self-love, and the courage to pursue your dreams. You are truly valuable, and the world is waiting to witness the remarkable contributions you have to offer.

I am worthy

Synonyms: deserving, meritorious, good, honest, laudable, reliable, noble, honorable

Worthy means deserving respect, admiration, attention, notice, or support; admired for good and useful qualities; fit or safe for; honorable; meritorious; commendable excellence or merit; having adequate character or value.

Worthy means deserving respect, admiration, attention, notice, or support; admired for good and useful qualities; fit or safe for; honorable; meritorious; commendable excellence or merit; having adequate character or value.

Understanding the difference between value and worthiness is crucial in cultivating a positive belief in your own worth. While value pertains to your contribution and your perception of your usefulness or importance, worthiness is about recognizing and embracing your inherent deservingness of love, respect, and acceptance simply by virtue of being human. It is a deeply rooted internal sense of self-acceptance and self-love independent of external validation or judgment.

Embracing your worthiness involves honoring your unique qualities and recognizing the nobility within yourself. Synonyms like meritorious, deserving, and noble capture the essence of worthiness and inspire a sense of pride and self-assurance. By acknowledging your worthiness, you can sit up a little straighter, embodying the confidence that comes from knowing you are deserving of love and respect.

It's natural to have concerns about feeling entitled in recognizing your own worth. But entitlement stems from the belief that life owes you something, often without considering the needs or perspectives of others. Worthiness is different. It is grounded in the intention to accept and love yourself, and it also extends to accepting and appreciating others. Cultivating worthiness involves nurturing self-acceptance, self-love, and gratitude. By embracing these qualities, your sense of worth will continue to grow, empowering you to live a more fulfilling and authentic life.

Remember, you are worthy, and your worthiness is not contingent upon external achievements or the opinions of others. Embrace your inherent value, set boundaries that honor your self-worth, and recognize the meritorious qualities that make you who you are. By cultivating a deep sense of worthiness, you can experience greater self-acceptance, genuine love for yourself, and a profound appreciation for the unique person you are.

I trust myself

Synonyms: honor, pleasure, delight, dignity, self-respect, certainty, commitment, belief, faith.

Trust means to believe someone is good and honest and will not harm you, or something is safe and reliable; to have confidence or a belief in someone; reliance on the integrity of a person; expect that something is true.

Trust is a powerful belief that forms the foundation of strong relationships and personal well-being. When you trust someone, you have faith in their goodness, honesty, and their commitment to not causing you harm. Similarly, trust can extend to safe and reliable things, providing a sense of security and dependability.

In the context of self-trust, it means having unwavering belief and confidence in yourself. It means relying on your own integrity and expecting that you will act in alignment with your values. When you trust yourself, you can depend on your ability to follow through on your commitments and make decisions that are true to who you are.

Building self-trust can bring about profound transformations in your life. Making decisions becomes much easier and less daunting when you have a strong sense of self-trust. Instead of second-guessing yourself or seeking constant validation from others, you can trust your own judgment and intuition. You become more attuned to your inner wisdom and have the courage to make choices that align with your authentic self.

Furthermore, cultivating self-trust involves treating yourself with kindness and compassion. When you extend understanding and forgiveness to yourself, even in times of mistakes or setbacks, you foster a sense of trust in your own resilience. You learn that you can rely on your own support and guidance, knowing you will have your own back no matter what.

Remember, you are deserving of trust, both from others and from yourself. Trust in your own capacity to make wise choices, act with integrity, and live a fulfilling and purposeful life. Trust that you have the resilience and resources to navigate the journey ahead and embrace the limitless potential within you. You trust yourself.

I have what it takes (I am capable)

Synonyms: able, accomplished, adept, experienced, efficient, gifted, proficient, skillful, qualified, talented, suited, good

Capable means being able to do things effectively and skillfully, and to achieve results; having attributes (such as physical or mental power) required for performance or accomplishment; having legal right to own, enjoy, or perform.

Being capable is a remarkable quality that encompasses effectiveness, skillfulness, and the ability to achieve desired results. It signifies possessing the necessary attributes, whether they are physical or mental, to perform tasks and accomplish goals. Saying "I have what it takes" carries an even greater impact than simply acknowledging your capabilities. It implies not only having the necessary skills but also possessing the determination and resilience to see things through to the end.

Embracing the belief that you have what it takes is a powerful affirmation of your inner strength and resourcefulness. It stems from a deep conviction within your heart that you can tackle any problem or challenge that comes your way. You understand that with sufficient time, research, and a willingness to try new approaches—even if they may not immediately succeed—you have the capacity to find solutions and overcome obstacles. This unwavering belief in your ability to navigate through difficulties is at the core of the "I have what it takes" mindset. You truly have what it takes.

Planting the positive belief of "I have what it takes" is about nurturing a mindset of confidence and self-assurance. It means trusting in your own capabilities and acknowledging that you possess the necessary tools to accomplish your goals. It involves recognizing your strengths, talents, and unique qualities that contribute to your ability to excel. By cultivating a sense of self-belief and perseverance, you can overcome self-doubt and rise above challenges with determination and resilience.

Remember, you are more capable than you may realize. Trust in your innate potential and your capacity to learn, adapt, and grow. Embrace the idea that you possess the skills, knowledge, and inner fortitude to tackle any endeavor that inspires you. By planting and nurturing the positive belief that "I have what it takes," you empower yourself to approach life's opportunities and challenges with unwavering confidence and a steadfast belief in your own abilities. You have what it takes.

What life looks like embodying these beliefs

When you begin to embody these seven core beliefs at varying levels, you may notice a slight reduction in striving, that feeling of struggling or fighting. Before I had recognized the weakness of some of these beliefs, especially "I am enough" and "I have what it takes," I set goals that proved to myself or others that these beliefs were true. It's like I didn't believe I am enough, but if I could just achieve this next level of success, then I would feel like I am enough.

Here's the sad truth: no amount of success will change your opinion of yourself. If you don't believe in yourself and you manage to claw and scratch and strive your way to creating a multi-million-dollar company, you won't believe in yourself. Victoria Song shares that she had clients who sold their billion-dollar company, and instead of feeling successful, they felt nothing. They weren't sad or unhappy; they weren't anything. They had numbed themselves to their pain at such a high level that they couldn't feel joy or love either.

Brooke Castillo teaches this concept that there is not better than here. If you believe when you get this thing (promotion, toy, etc.) or accomplish this goal, then you'll relax, love yourself, whatever. When you get there, then you'll slow down. There is not better than here. There is worth pursuing for your evolution and for different experiences, but not to feel something different. If you want to feel something different, you have to choose a new thought, literally choose a new response.

I found a very cool resource that explains some options for choosing new responses and, along the way also, helps understand and label the feelings you are having. Paul Ekman, a psychologist and leading researcher on emotions, surveyed more than 100 scientists and used their input to develop what's known as the Atlas of Emotions. His website www.atlasofemotions.org proposes five main categories of emotions: anger, fear, sadness, disgust, and enjoyment. Doesn't this sound remarkably like the five characters in Pixar's Inside Out?

This website also lays out how emotions work. First, there's the timeline which begins with a trigger. There's a scenario that shows you how if a friend gets angry with you, your different emotions have different results. After a trigger, you experience the physical sensations impacting your view of the situation. Then we have an opportunity to respond. Jack Canfield talks about responsibility as literally a combination of the words response and ability. Our ability to respond.

As we complete emotional cycles for these core beliefs, you may find that you actually don't choose a response. Often, completing the cycle removes the trigger, so someone can say something that has typically upset you. Now it doesn't register as a problem because they aren't confirming your belief about yourself.

Completing the emotional cycles for these core beliefs will create a deeper sense of feeling like you are already there. There's tension between the concept of I've arrived, AND I hope I'll be even better tomorrow. As Victoria Song says, one foot in gratitude and one foot in hopeful expectation.

Integrating trauma

You are now equipped to decide what a sensation means in the moment and process previously incomplete emotional cycles. However, sometimes we still have pretty vivid memories of the trauma we experienced. The memories may fade, but if not, you may need to complete a process psychologists call integrating your trauma. Remember, trauma is anything that happens to you that your mind can't make sense of. This means part of the healing process involves moving from your body into your mind. To do that, we need to begin to organize the stories and make sense of them.

Here's the great news: it can happen faster than you think. Bessel van der Kolk discusses this healing with the caveat that often, talk therapy isn't required. If you let your body complete the cycle, you don't have to spend years discussing how crappy your childhood was. Again, if you had major trauma, your nervous system often won't stay regulated long enough for you to feel this stuff without some assistance from a trained professional. But can I get a cheer for "Maybe I only need a little therapy instead of a lifetime of therapy"?

The first step to integrating your trauma is to look at the story you've told yourself about your trauma. How did you originally "make sense" of the situation? Said another way, "What buggy files did you create to protect yourself in the future?" You've heard the saying; history isn't what happened to you. It's what you believe about what happened to you. If you were abandoned, you might have created the story that everyone always leaves eventually. You may have used that story to decide you won't let anyone get super close to you anymore. This story protected you, but you may now be able to see that it left you lonely. Safe, but alone. It has worked for you, but is it what you want in the future?

Next is to acknowledge the pain or trauma caused. Sometimes this is as simple as saying that it was really hard. For me, I had discounted how hard things were because I survived them. Later I'll talk about developing self-compassion and how my daughter helped with that, but at this point, know that your heart, especially the little kid that still lives inside of you, wants someone to scoop them up and say, "That sucked, it was really hard, and I see you."

After acknowledging how hard something was, the next step may seem counterintuitive. It is to find what came out of the situation that has served you. I used to say, find the good, but when you've had significant trauma, that feels belittling. You developed coping skills that have served you. Because of the traumatic things that happened to me, I discovered I have a high capacity to survive really hard things, I developed the skill of perseverance, I developed compassion for people who are treated badly, I have a finely tuned sense of humor because I needed humor to survive some of the crap, I could go on and on. Am I glad those things happened to me?? F*@#$ no! Do I wish I could have developed these coping skills without the trauma? F#$% yes! However, what someone else intended for destruction, I've learned to find what strengths and skills I got from the situation. This has allowed me to not stay in victim mode because I know I can control my emotions, my responses, my thoughts, and the stories I tell myself. For those of us who hated how out-of-control childhood trauma made us feel, I love these types of control since they allow me to create the life I want.

Keeping a right-sized view of the situation

Things happened to you, and you get to decide what it means. Period, the end. Years ago, my friend was in therapy. Money was tight, so she and I decided that when one or the other was in therapy, we would get more value if we shared what we had learned. It was like 2-for-1. She shared a story she felt was truly tragic. Her therapist replied, "That's unfortunate." He said that labeling something as tragic gave it a lot more weight in our brains. We'd like our children to do what we ask, but it's unfortunate when they don't. We'd like our husbands to wash clothes or dishes, but it's unfortunate that it doesn't always happen. A small tweak to the words we use can change our perception of something. A situation can go from terrible, awful, rotten, and no-good to just unfortunate. This is not to minimize your feelings. It's actually designed to balance your emotions and give your nervous system a break from its fight-or-flight default.

How feeling your emotions change the role of the inner critic

As you learn to feel your emotions, you may notice that the voices in your head, the committee assisting your inner critic, begins to get confused. You may have believed for a long time that you weren't good enough, and you tried everything to change that belief or numb the pain around that belief. You develop coping skills with the help of your inner critic to keep you safe, as we talked about previously.

As you are learning to feel your emotions and reduce the toxic waste, your inner critic may get louder initially because your inner critic has come to believe that the only effective protection is to crack the whip. If it can keep you running harder and faster, then it can potentially protect you. As you become more aware of this inner critic, you will begin to see how this inner critic is saying terribly mean things to you. When clients tell me what they say to themselves, I ask if they would say that about their best friend. If not, then don't say it to yourself. You may not share my faith perspective, but I'm here to tell you that God did not make junk; we all make mistakes.

As you get to know this inner critic, you might think you're just supposed to tell it to shut up and get out of there.

But I would propose to you that the inner critic has been doing its job very well. It has been keeping you safe. It has been watching out for your survival. And if you try to just kick it to the curb, it's not really going to be super effective. Number one, it's scary. Because you feel like you're ditching all the protective tools that you have. But number two, it just doesn't work because the inner critic will fight kicking and screaming. Your brain's survival mechanism will override your best plans and dreams.

And so, if you can imagine the voices in your head as a board of directors, one member of the board is the part of you that wants you to be courageous, and there's another member that's the part of you that wants you to be safe. One member wants to love really well, while another member says, "No, no, no. When you love people, and you get too close, then they're going to hurt you." If you consider the board in your head, you can imagine that your inner critic has been the board chair and a little bit of a dictator up until now.

In the movie Inside Out, there's a whole sequence of the movie where the character Joy has been running the control panel for Riley. Then Joy gets sucked out of headquarters, and suddenly the panel is being run by the other emotions, everything from fear to disgust to anger. That's kind of the way the concept of the inner critic is, and you've allowed them to be at the controls for a very long time.

Instead of kicking the inner critic off of the board, I'm going to invite you to ask them to just move out of the board chair position and into a board member position.

When you ask the inner critic to leave the board chair position, you thank them for their service and for all the years they've kept you safe. You ask them to just be a member of the board because you now want a new board chair. The new board chair is Adult You, with dreams, aspirations, and the ability to make decisions based on facts and emotions, not just on the past. There's a voice in your head that represents the inner child who wants to speak up for the courageous, compassionate, and curious you. You want that voice to take a larger role now.

I find it helpful to me to actually assign names to those voices. Perhaps you call the inner critic Negative Nelly, and maybe the compassionate version of you is Caring Cathy. Sometimes I have clients that will use the name of their childhood bully as the name for their inner critic, like "Oh my gosh, the mean girl when I was in seventh grade was Ashley or Britney," or whatever. Then they will give a positive version of themselves and maybe like a sweet teacher. One of my favorite teachers was Susie. Perhaps Sweet Susie is the name of my compassionate, caring version of me.

When you are in this transition, just like when a leadership change happens on a board, then every policy that has been decided up to now needs to be reviewed. This means that the way we've always done things isn't how we're going to do them in the future. Just like when an organization is going through a change –– whether it's a software upgrade or a new personnel policy –– you know that it takes time, and you've got to get everybody to buy in.

It's so easy to just default to the inner critic, but you have to begin to slow down and take time to listen to the compassionate, curious view. The voice that isn't going to judge you but will say things like, "Oh, that makes sense that you would feel that way." This takes a lot of self-awareness. The definition of self-awareness is noticing the impact your behavior has on others. I think self-awareness is also noticing how your actions do or don't align with your internal standards.

You may have to literally do things you've never done before. I'm not a huge journaler, but during the period when I was trying to slow down my thoughts, I could take a moment and write down all of the thoughts that were bouncing through my head. I could either write them down or say them out loud. There's an app called Marco Polo that allows you to send video chats to people, and I have a dear, sweet friend who is willing to listen to me when there's a bunch of thoughts flying around my brain. I can literally go on Marco Polo and press record, and I can just word-vomit all the things that are going on in my head. Frequently, this allows me to see the thoughts and realize, "Oh wow, that's my brain trying to keep me safe because this seems so similar to another situation when I was younger and got hurt." If I can't see it, then my sweet friend can sometimes notice things I didn't.

I know I'm very blessed to have friends that will do that. You can also just record yourself, sharing your thoughts with yourself. You can use journaling, whatever it takes to begin noticing what you say to yourself when things don't go well.

In the beginning, this may be really tiring. I mean, I'm not going to sugarcoat it. It's just tiring. But just like when we learn how to ride a bike, we fall down a lot. We just kept trying because we knew we wanted to ride a bike. I'm just telling you to just keep trying. It's worth the investment to travel lighter and live with more peace.

Revisiting your motives

Lots of things shift when you're able to complete emotional loops -- and your motives are one of them. Now that I've completed so many of my previous outstanding emotional loops, I can see that some of my goal-setting was actually done to combat the negative beliefs I had about myself. Might it be the same for you?

As we've discussed, when you set goals without knowing the negative beliefs in play, you end up with a goal designed to prove the negative belief wrong. So, you might set a revenue goal with an unconscious motivation to try to prove that you are valuable. "When I make this much money, my dad will have to accept that I am successful," that kind of thing. Here's the unfortunate truth. Without processing that emotion, you will never prove it to yourself or anyone else.

After you have set goals in whatever style you prefer, I encourage you to test your emotional cycles against the seven core beliefs discussed above. One question that Byron

Katie recommends in her book Loving What Is has really been helping me uncover residual emotions: "Is this true?"

My process is the following:

First, I write down the goal I have set. For instance, I will earn X dollars as a coach, author, and speaker this year. Goal-setting experts will say this isn't specific enough since it doesn't have a date, but it's what I'm working with in this new gentle space I'm cultivating for myself.

After I write the goal, I write the first belief in positive current language. I am enough.

Next, I state the goal. Then I ask myself, is this true? Yes or no. I will earn X dollars as a coach, author, and speaker this year. I am enough. (Ask: is this true?)

This next step is critical. I state the goal and then ask myself, is there any part of me that doesn't believe this? Yes or no. I sit and think quietly and listen to what thoughts come up.

Then, I work through each belief in positive form with the two follow-up questions – is it true, and is there any part of me that doesn't believe this?
- I am lovable
- I belong
- I am enough
- I am valuable
- I am worthy
- I trust myself
- I have what it takes

When I asked myself these questions for the revenue goal I set, then quietly sat with each question, I got to "I trust myself." Instead of yes or no answers, a whole list of questions came up.
- Can I trust myself to not be a workaholic?
- Can I trust myself to honor my commitments?
- Can I trust myself to be authentic?
- Can I trust myself to manage my money?
- Can I trust myself to have a lot of fun?

These answers allowed me to pause, sit with myself and listen to my body and what it wanted to tell me. I had to feel the sensations in my body that these questions brought up. What came up was in this new era of learning to feel my emotions and be gentler with myself, I found I didn't have a long track record of success. If the goal required grinding it out and doing whatever it took, I had confidence and a lot of examples of success. What I had to resolve myself with was I trusted myself to choose this more peaceful path each day. I knew I had been able to accomplish amazing things in short periods of time while working with peace. I had to rest my confidence in this.

These questions gave me a starting point for making contingency plans while pursuing the goal. I could be more aware of the potential pitfalls and create guardrails to prevent getting too far off course. They can do the same for you, so give it a try. But remember, this is a tricky area because I think you have to know yourself, be really honest with yourself, and be willing to be super gentle with yourself. So go slow, use the tools learned so far in this book to keep yourself grounded and close emotional loops as they come up.

To sum up:

Before, you had toxic barrels of negative beliefs, and it seemed like you only had a hand shovel to dig out the weeds, so it seemed to take forever. We've been upgrading your tools so that you can use power tools to do massive renewal quickly. I believe these positive forms of those beliefs are like planting a garden with a continuous supply of fruits and vegetables. You will continue to reap the benefits for many years. One remarkable outcome of releasing the need to constantly prove yourself is the profound sense of peace it brings. Without the weight of constantly striving for validation, you'll find yourself infused with newfound energy to set and achieve your goals. Furthermore, we've equipped you with a technique to assess your motives when setting goals, enabling you to uncover areas that require emotional closure and resolution. As we delve into the next phase of developing a harmonious relationship with yourself, you'll utilize all the tools we've been carefully adding to your toolbox. You'll discover that hand tools are sometimes necessary, while power tools are more suitable at other times. As you continue to refine these skills, you'll gain the wisdom to discern which tool to apply in each situation, maximizing your personal growth and transformation.

CHAPTER 8
Building a relationship with yourself

In the previous chapters, we've covered important topics like planting new beliefs, easing the pressure to constantly strive, and reevaluating the role of your inner critic. Now, let's dive deeper into a crucial aspect of your personal growth: developing a new and healthier relationship with yourself. This entails building a foundation of self-care and self-love rather than the toxic beliefs that may have hindered your progress. It's essential to recognize the significance of grief and forgiveness when beginning this journey. Just as in any relationship that needs rebuilding, your relationship with yourself requires a similar process. While you've processed some of your emotions, now you have to grant yourself permission to grieve for any pain, disappointments, or unfulfilled expectations you may have experienced.

Grieving and forgiving yourself for how things have been

In this process of learning how to feel your emotions, there may be things that come up to make you realize that you have hurt you have been unable to let go of. You literally haven't been able to forgive them, so I want to talk about that for a moment.

For starters, forgiveness is to release others and not hold them accountable. Literally to give them a presidential pardon, even if they don't ask for forgiveness. When you forgive someone, it does not condone what they did. When you forgive others, it also does not mean you have to restore the relationship.

It took me 10 years to forgive my stepdad for his sexual abuse of me when I was a teenager. It took 25 years for him to ask for forgiveness. Even after he asked for forgiveness, I told him, "I forgave you 15 years ago. I had to for myself." He wanted to jump right back into a relationship, and I wasn't ready for that. I actually had a really hard time trusting him. I had daughters, and I just wasn't willing to be in a relationship with someone who had spent most of my life denying my reality. It was just too much and too hard. We never really restored the relationship before he died. We got to a place where he sent me some encouraging words about my first book and encouraged me to keep telling the truth and my story, which is kind of miraculous since my story involved his abuse. That doesn't mean I didn't forgive him. I actually really encouraged him to forgive himself. He said, "I don't know how I could ever do that." I totally understand. When you forgive others who have caused you pain, then you can almost come to a point with enough therapy that you can decide, "Oh, OK, I see how they were doing the best they could based on their skills, the culture they were raised in or their own pain" or "I can see how this was not a malicious attempt."

When someone hurts you, it may cause perpetual damage to you. I believe that each time your life is affected by that damage, you may have to forgive them again.

For instance, because of what my stepdad did, for the first 5-8 years of our marriage, sometimes, when my husband patted my butt in the kitchen playfully or walked in to talk to me while I was in the shower, I would completely freak out. Not every time, but sometimes. I would explore why I freaked out and determine it was related to the lack of sexual safety and physical autonomy I had with my stepdad. I would get really frustrated because I thought I had already dealt with it in therapy. I hadn't learned about nervous system response and completing emotional cycles. I did come to realize that I had to forgive him each time my life was different as a consequence of his action. I think this is what Jesus meant when he said to forgive your brother 70 times seven. (Though I don't think he was telling us to keep going into abusive situations because Psalms tells us to guard our heart for it is the well-spring of life.)

But what about when you turn this same process toward yourself? You can potentially explain or reason your way through why someone else may have done the things they did. But man, when you have to forgive yourself for your own choices that caused your own self pain. Ah, it is so much more challenging. On top of that, you have to be willing to forgive yourself for how you've treated yourself after making poor decisions.

In April of 2021, I was Facebook Live journaling my journey through grief, and I had one day I was just overwhelmed with how angry I was at myself over my health journey. Since I'd had kids, I had believed I was too tall to be a size four or size six. If I ever lost enough weight to be a size eight, I was ecstatic. Wow, that was amazing.

Most of the time, I was size 10 or 12, and I worked hard to not go a lot higher than that. There were definitely seasons of my life when I inched up to a size 14, then I would start exercising more, start eating better, and just yo-yo-ed back and forth. But I honestly believed I could not be smaller than a size eight. I was just too tall.

Then I went on my health journey, and I lost weight. This could sound very superficial, but it's my reality as I lost nearly 30 pounds. I got all the way down to a size two at one point. When I went and bought those new jeans that were size two, I was unbelievably annoyed at myself because I realized that I had just decided and limited myself for all those years, believing this was just the way it was. Weirdly, I felt betrayed. I felt like I had lied to myself for 20 years. And honestly, it felt dumb.

It was such an interesting experience to see this betrayal of myself by myself. And to figure out what to do with the sensations when I thought about lying to myself for all those years. I was angry. It was super tempting to let my inner critic beat up on me. However, I was already figuring out this wasn't very effective. I sometimes got mad at myself that I didn't see it until then, though. How did I not see it? I guess Dorothy spent the whole movie wearing the shoes that would have got her home. I finally had to realize that this was my ruby slippers moment, and I had the answer the whole time. I just didn't know I had the answer. So, I had to forgive myself. Forgive myself for my choices, the lies I told myself, and the things I had done to survive. I had to forgive myself for everything.

Learning to work with self-judgment

All of this protection and lying to ourselves leads to a LOT of self-judgment. It seemed to be my inner critic's favorite tool. So, if we want to eliminate self-judgments, what we have to develop is self-compassion.

Self-compassion is a powerful concept that begins with the simple act of noticing your pain. It requires you to come out of denial and stop turning a blind eye to the discomfort you're experiencing. It's time to break free from the habit of ignoring your pain, as that only perpetuates your suffering. By acknowledging and accepting the presence of pain in your life, you take the first step toward self-compassion.

Once you've noticed your pain, the next important aspect is genuinely being moved by it. This means allowing yourself to be emotionally touched by your own struggles rather than dismissing them with phrases like "Suck it up, buttercup." Being moved by your pain involves recognizing its significance and the challenges it poses. It requires a compassionate response that acknowledges the difficulty of your circumstances. By allowing yourself to be moved by your pain, you open the door to self-compassion and begin to cultivate a deeper understanding and empathy for yourself.

Lastly, it's vital to understand that pain, failure, and rejection are an inherent part of the human experience. Instead of fearing or avoiding these aspects of life, it's essential to recognize their inevitability. By acknowledging that pain is a natural and normal occurrence, you can begin to challenge the automatic response of your inner critic. Your inner critic tends to categorize all pain as leading to a metaphorical death, making it seem overwhelming and unbearable. However, by accepting the inevitability of pain, you can allow yourself to respond with self-compassion, understanding that it is a part of the human journey and doesn't define your worth or your future.

In summary, self-compassion is a multi-step process that involves noticing your pain, being moved by it, and acknowledging the universality of pain, failure, and rejection. By embracing self-compassion, you can free yourself from denial, embrace your emotions with empathy, and release the harsh judgments imposed by your inner critic. It is through self-compassion that you can cultivate a deeper sense of understanding, acceptance, and kindness towards yourself as you navigate the ups and downs of life.

With all the hurt that I had in childhood, I endured it by denying how hard it was. It was a great technique to survive. Apparently, ignoring the pain was OK because I did survive. When it came time to notice my pain and be moved by it, I processed it most effectively as my daughter reached the age I had been when I experienced the pain and loss. Ironically, when Sami was eight, I was 29, which is the same ages my adopted mom and I were when she died of cancer. As I looked at eight-year-old Sami and thought, "Oh my goodness. How freaking hard would it be for Sami to lose her mom at this age?" Wow. It gave me an opportunity to see my own pain by imagining how hard it would be for my daughter.

Barry's a fantastic dad; he would have jumped in with both feet. Sami had family support, and she had all my friends who would have totally been there for her. And it would have still been hard for her. My dad had left a few months before my mom died, and she didn't have many friends left after years of moving around. She had family members, but there were just such a small number of people to provide support for me.

Yet I had ignored that pain for years and years and treated it like it was no big deal because I survived. What's interesting is that now with my grandson, I'm learning a whole new level of self-compassion. I'm learning how to talk to myself using way more gentle language. I would love to tell you that I learned to speak gently with my children, but quite frankly, I had not healed enough. My perfectionism and protection meant I needed my kids to be OK, so that I seemed OK. I still had expectations for them. I made how they behaved mean something about me. (Because, remember, our brain loves to make sense of things.) I still have to be careful to not make how my daughter parents her children mean something about me. Maybe you can relate? I wonder if that's why grandparents constantly comment on their children's parenting, and it sounds so much like judgment.

But when I talk to my grandson, I now have the wisdom of all these years. I have the wisdom of surviving all of my children's childhoods and recognizing that they're going to make choices that have nothing to do with me. With him, I can see how it is much easier to speak gently to him. Am I perfect? No. Is it helpful that my daughter has a degree in communication, is a huge believer in gentle parenting, and provides tips and tricks? Yes.

So, maybe you don't have children, and maybe you don't have grandchildren, in which case I would love to invite you to use your imagination. It's a fabulous tool that we talked about earlier. So, if you imagine something that happened to you when you were young and now that is happening to perhaps one of your co-worker's 10-year-old daughters. Maybe she felt left out because her friends didn't invite her to the sleepover, and she happened to be at your office?

Would you tell her to suck it up, buttercup? No! You would tell her, "Oh, man. Feeling left out is hard." You might say some funny things like, "Oh, they're going to grow up and be ugly." I don't know. Sometimes we say funny things when trying to help kids get over feeling left out. But you wouldn't tell her to suck it up, buttercup. So, why would you tell yourself that?

Recognizing the pain can be as simple as saying, "Yeah, okay, so, what happened in the past is the past? But it hurt a lot." Pausing to acknowledge the pain is a huge step. Then we accept that in this life, there will be trouble and pain. The pain from the past taught us many lessons including, how to evolve, how to assess situations to determine people who aren't safe, and how to keep moving forward. But now, I want to do more than survive. I want to thrive.

Moving from self-judgment to self-compassion

As we develop self-compassion, we reduce self-judgment. Self-judgment is a favorite tool of my inner critic to keep me "in line", doing things it deems safe. As a board member, instead of the board chair, the inner critic can be transformed into a board member who shows caution and can ask good questions. For instance, if you want to quit your job and start an underwater basket-weaving business, your cautious board member (former inner critic) could ask, "Have you thought about paying off all of your debt? Have you thought about having a savings account as a cushion? Have you thought about perhaps getting a part-time job at a coffee shop that gives you enough money to be able to pay your bills while you develop your new business so you keep a regulated nervous system?"

In this case, the cautious board member might actually have some words of wisdom for you. This could be helpful if they're asking questions and not beating you over the head. Now, if they start beating you over the head, you could say, "Thank you for your feedback. Please take your seat."

Curiosity

All of this requires you to get to know yourself. There's one more tool I want to talk about when getting to know yourself, and that is curiosity. It turns out that if your brain does not feel safe, it will not allow you to be curious. If a lion is chasing you in the jungle, you won't be curious about what kind of cool flower it is you're running by. You're just going to run.

So, part of what you have to do to be able to allow yourself to be curious is to get your nervous system calmed down as you've been practicing. You have to allow yourself to meet yourself with curiosity instead of self-judgment because, remember, judgment was just you forming an opinion based on available evidence and material. Curiosity allows us to collect more evidence and collect more material.

As you're going through this process and becoming more self-aware when you do something wrong, an alternative to beating yourself up would be to say, "Hmm, that's so interesting. Why did I go back to that same way of dealing with the situation?" You could ask curious questions, like,

- Am I feeling tired?
- Am I feeling hungry?
- Am I feeling overwhelmed?
- Do I feel safe?

What can I do to increase my safety right now to allow me to act in a way that is in alignment with my values?

Occasionally, you may experience reluctance when it comes to delving deeper into self-discovery. It's understandable to feel a sense of fear or apprehension about truly getting to know yourself. You might worry that the lies you've been telling yourself are actually true, causing you to question your own identity. It's also possible to feel a certain unease about being fully present in your own body. But here's the reassuring truth: it's perfectly okay to have these feelings. Despite the doubts and uncertainties, you have already shown great strength and resilience by navigating through life's challenges. Take a moment to acknowledge and appreciate yourself for making it this far. Your ability to endure and persevere is truly commendable. Keep up the good work!

And it doesn't have to be that way anymore. You can slowly but surely get to know yourself. If you don't know how, think about when you are getting to know another person. Tell me about yourself. Tell me about where you come from. What makes you tick? Who are you? What's your story? And then listen and decide if that's the story you really want to tell about yourself. Is there a different version of the story?

I can remember I used to be so embarrassed by the fact that in second grade, I had gotten paddlings seemingly every day. Yes, corporal punishment was a thing in the South in 1981. When I didn't complete my work, I would have to miss recess. If I still didn't complete my work, I would get paddled. It wasn't until years later, when working through a concern that I wasn't good at working hard that this memory came up. I realized the semester when I did so poorly in school and got paddled nearly every day was the same semester my mom died. I had to say, "Of course, you weren't focused. Of course, you weren't able to concentrate and get your homework done. You were afraid because your dad left, and you didn't know where you were going when your mom died." I had to get to know myself. Get to know my story. Then figure out if that was the version of the story I wanted to believe about myself.

Shifting self-judgment: what's the story?

We all naturally judge ourselves: we compare ourselves to each other and form opinions about ourselves based on our perceptions of them. That tracks so far, right? But here's the thing most people don't realize. In making that comparison between yourself and the other person, you're not working from a neutral, objective view of yourself. (Or them, for that matter!) You're making the comparison based on your previous experiences and underlying beliefs. This is why it's important to start investigating the stories you're telling yourself -- because once you start uncovering what's really at play, you can shift your perspective and start relating with yourself from a place of deeper love and care.

Imagine for a moment that you have a friend who makes illogical decisions. (At least, they seem illogical from your perspective.) They plan to meet you for dinner, then don't show up and don't call. They agree to help you with a project but then go out with their new boyfriend instead. They go radio silent for weeks. Then when they finally call you, they tell you all about how awful life their is and all their difficulties.

None of this makes sense without the backstory. Perhaps their dad left their mom without any money, and they suffered without food. Then their mom's next four husbands did the exact same thing. For them, losing a boyfriend equals losing all safety and could leave them without food. Consequently, in choosing between spending time with a new boyfriend or following through on the promises to you, they choose the boyfriend, unconsciously believing in your understanding nature.

From the perspective of choices, "I will upset my friend" or "I won't have food", it makes sense that they would bail on you. This behavior served them in the past to survive, but they may need an upgrade now to establish more authentic relationships. And you do the exact same thing! We all have old stories and patterns that no longer serve us. One of my long-time favorites was "I'm clumsy." I told that story for years!

I found evidence everywhere to provide confirmation of clumsy and not strong labels. During their elementary years, I enjoyed church camp with my kids and often returned home hurt. In toilet tag, when tagged, you freeze, kneel down with one knee on the ground, one knee up, and your hand in the air as the chain. To unfreeze you, someone on your team "sits" on your knee and "pulls the chain." I was playing and got tagged. While frozen, a 6'6" dad squatted on my knee and then very quickly flung his elbow into my forehead to pull the chain. It literally broke the skin on my forehead. I cried all the way to the nurse irrationally, saying, "My husband told me to be careful because I get really competitive around my friend Dana, and she's my age with four kids and much more naturally athletic than I am!" Another time, while racing Dana on a bungee run, I reached out as far as I could to get the bag farther out than she did. When the bungee cord snapped back, I hit the bounce lane directly on my neck. Pretty close to a concussion based on the next hour worth of dizziness. This identity of being clumsy, not strong, and not a good athlete held me back. When I ran, it hurt. I believed hurting meant I shouldn't run very far. I didn't know that sometimes when you work out, your body hurts.

Imagine there have been two movie crews following you throughout your life. One has been capturing moments/evidence proving your negative beliefs of not being lovable or valuable are true. The other crew has been capturing moments/evidence to prove the positive beliefs of you being lovable and valuable are true. As the director and main star of the movie of your life, you have the opportunity to go back into the editing room and revise the movie so that you notice the positive beliefs, and you leave the "evidence" to prove the negative beliefs on the cutting room floor. This will create a movie and life journey to serves you and create more peace, joy, and freedom than ever before while reducing self-judgment.

Know yourself

As I've mentioned, all this involves a willingness to know yourself. You may say, "Yo Angela, I don't know about you, but I spend 24 hours a day with myself." I would reply, "How much time do you spend alone without distraction? How much of the time do you turn off the music, put down the phone, turn off the TV, and just sit with yourself?"

To begin with, it may only be three minutes, but just like any other form of exercise, you can build up stamina. Often, we think we should go from zero to 60 when we start meditating or anything new. Too harsh. Just as you wouldn't walk into the gym and try to lift 300 lbs. on your first day, take it slow when starting a new routine, like learning to sit with yourself and tune into your body.

When I was commuting to work, I made a conscious choice to not wear headphones so I could be more fully present. I didn't want music or podcasts to distract me from my thoughts. I often prayed, "What are we going to talk about today, Lord?" This allowed me to begin a practice of being alone with my thoughts, and I began to notice little things going on in my body. Time and again, I found that being able to ride my bike without distractions created comfort in knowing my body and becoming comfortable being alone with my own mind.

Remember how I talked about doing something physical while you begin to learn to calm your nervous system? Here's another example. Think about first dates. You don't typically sit there and stare at each other. Instead, you go get coffee, have a meal, play mini-golf, or something. By having something physical to do, you take the pressure off and can get to know the other person. Works for yourself as well.

When I got comfortable being alone with myself and my own thoughts, one unexpected benefit was being able to come up with different solutions to hard problems. I had spent a lot of time thinking that taking time to experience my emotions would make me less effective, softer, I don't know, less of who I was at my core. Instead, I found more energy available that I had been using to hold the emotions at bay. When my mind is quiet, and I cultivate curiosity, seemingly impossible problems suddenly have many additional alternatives. For me, this applied to everything from restructuring a department that wasn't working to using a different response when one of my adult children wanted to remind me of the ways I hadn't been the parent they wanted when they were growing up. Being able to sit with yourself and be alone with your thoughts may cause you apprehension, but wade in and stick with it to discover the extra benefits you'll find.

Forming your committee of wisdom

Another key element of loving yourself and developing a relationship of self-care is learning how to work with yourself when you're feeling resistance. Most of us habitually push right through it -- play through the pain! But this may not be kind or loving. Instead, you need to learn to invite all the parts of yourself to the table, so to speak, so you can gently work with yourself and move through the resistance.

I often do this with clients who don't fully believe they can achieve a new goal. Let's say the goal is to launch their new life coaching practice. Typically, there's a part of them that believes this is possible especially as they are finishing certification. But if I pick up on a slight hesitation, like when they imagine introducing themselves at a networking event, I encourage them to sit with the committee in their head. There's a part of them that believes fully 100% this is going to be great; this is the part of us we access when we choose a new thought.

But there's a part of them that doesn't believe it. Now, most of the time, we try to blow past this part of ourselves and tell it to sit down and shut up, or at least be quiet. But self-love and self-care include your whole self -- not just the convenient parts.

So, in my session with that client, I would say, "The part of you that believes this is true gets the most time at the microphone because, as a life coach, it's off-brand to think negatively. Let's listen to the part of you that doesn't believe it's true."

People have to quiet themselves to begin to hear this. I encourage them to think the thought they are trying to believe: "I am a successful life coach." Then explore where in their body the lack of belief shows up as sensations. This is critical to success. To clear this lack of belief, you have to notice the sensation and allow it to give you information, before you ca n release it. It takes a lot of self-control to allow something unpleasant and even more to just sit with it while you wait for it to give you information. . (As you now know, after working with your feelings yourself!)

We literally spend time allowing and being grateful for it, not trying to change it. Then we begin the process you've learned of noticing, zooming in, describing, and then finally handing it a microphone. The most common thing which comes up when the part of you that doesn't believe you can achieve the goal gets the microphone is it wants you to make a plan and not fly by the seat of your pants. So we reassure that part that we will make a plan and we will develop contingencies for when Plan A doesn't work, as well as reassuring it that we will not beat ourselves up if it doesn't work. How much more loving is that than trying to force it into compliance or silence?

When you're able to shift those patterns, you'll find that your motivation to do something comes from love, and your desire to accomplish your goals is stronger than any kind of motivation you might have to avoid being yelled at by your inner critical voice. Many people think they need to continue to "should" on themselves and listen to the critical voice that tells them what to do so they can stay motivated, but this just isn't true.

As the board chair of an organization, Adult You gets to help set the agenda for the meetings of your committee of wisdom of all the parts of you when you are trying to make a decision. You get to decide how long the discussion is open. You get to decide which voices get lifted. This organization is your brain. It's time to take a more active leadership role.

There's a powerful addition I often encourage my clients to make to their personal board of directors — their future self. Together, we embark on a visualization exercise, transporting their minds to a future point in time where they can meet and converse with their wiser, more experienced selves. It's a remarkable journey, and I usually suggest two critical moments for this encounter: their 90th birthday or their deathbed. Unsurprisingly, many find the birthday scenario more accessible and comforting.

The inspiration for this practice came to me when I attended my dear friend Doris's 90th birthday celebration. Doris is the grandmother of my friend Julie, who relocated to our area when Julie's girls were just toddlers. Oh, the timing of it all—Julie discovered she was pregnant barely an hour before witnessing the miraculous birth of my youngest child, Lexi. What an unexpected surprise awaited her!

Over the years, Doris became not only a pillar of support for Julie but also for my youngest child. There was a semester when Josh had football practice at the exact same time Lexi had soccer in a neighboring town. Every Thursday during that semester, Doris graciously picked Lexi up from school, lending her a helping hand.

As I joined the gathering for Doris's 90th birthday party, I was struck by the diverse mix of attendees. Julie's youngest daughter's friend group was there, ranging from fourteen-year-olds to Doris's own small church community of "young people" in their 70s. Doris possesses an incredible gift for connecting with others—she loves people deeply, and her life experiences have rendered her a captivating conversationalist. Even at her age, Doris remains a devoted student of the Bible, recently undergoing the profound act of baptism. She embodies the essence of a lifelong learner. Whenever I speak about living to be 90, it is Doris who comes to mind—a shining example of a life lived fully.

Now, let's ignite your imagination. Close your eyes and envision the gathering for your own 90th birthday party. Who surrounds you in celebration? What kind of person have you become? Take a moment to clarify this vision in your mind.

Once you have a clear picture of your future self, consider inviting them to join the team of voices within your mind. They are the embodiment of wisdom and guidance, ready to offer invaluable insights as you navigate life's twists and turns. In my own experience, my 90-year-old self often reminds me not to take life too seriously, urging me to embrace the present moment and to love wholeheartedly.

But let's not stop there. There's another remarkable addition you can make to your internal board of directors—your future self who has already accomplished the very goal you've set out to achieve. They stand as a victorious testament, possessing intimate knowledge of the path you must walk. When you find a quiet moment to connect with this wise future self, you'll be amazed by the surge of inspiration that washes over you, guiding you toward the ideas and actions necessary to bring your goals to fruition.

Embracing the wisdom and guidance of your future selves grants you access to a wealth of insights, propelling you forward on your journey toward fulfillment and accomplishment. So, dare to dream, embrace the possibilities, and let the voices of your future selves guide you along the path to success.

Love your neighbor as yourself

It is said that the greatest commandment is to love your neighbor as yourself. It seems that many people stop after their neighbors. I think the real wisdom is in the word as. When we don't love ourselves, we spend our lives judging ourselves and having unreasonable expectations. And we can't seem to help how we treat others. We put our unreasonable expectations on them as well. How we talk to others is sometimes mild compared to how horribly we talk to ourselves. However, when you love yourself, accept your faults, and become gentle with your expectations, you will be able to do the same for others.

We see this in sports a lot. A coach thinks they will get more from their team by yelling at them all the time, constantly making them feel like they aren't good enough, and punishing them for every mistake. However, coaches who learn to show their team how much they care and push their team to be their best from a place of love can take average athletes and get top performance. These coaches often can work their teams harder than the coach that yells at them. Gratitude, love, and encouragement produce better results than belittling, condemnation, and shame do.

If someone tells me that they want to work on not judging others, I tell them not to bother. Instead, work on not judging themselves and loving themselves more Then naturally, you'll judge others less and love others better.

Abandonment, and one way this process worked for me

As we discussed in chapter three, many of us have experienced significant abandonment. As you learn to complete emotional cycles and notice sensations in your body, you are learning to not abandon yourself. This is a critical aspect of developing a relationship with yourself. Trust is built on being there for yourself. It's also imperative to accept all the parts of yourself and not try to get rid of the parts that aren't convenient or have been hurt in the past. For me, despite years of healing including, plenty of therapy, spiritual healing, and even writing a book about personal development, abandonment issues caught me completely off guard. In 2019, Barry and I began seeing a marriage therapist. About a year into the process, I remember our therapist, Ryan, nonchalantly said, "Angela, you will need to address your abandonment issues." Excuse me, my what? I didn't know I had an issue with a diagnosis code; I thought of the idiosyncrasies as features of my personality.

A few days later, I was riding my bike to work, thinking about this whole concept of abandonment. I was asking myself and God a series of questions, and suddenly my imagination got sparked, and a whole scenario played out in my head.

I imagined a little girl sitting on the makeshift porch of a trailer. Her name is Jenny. Sitting next to her is a grown-up woman.

For a long time, Jenny has been yelling at this woman to do better, be better, and speak up for people who can't speak for themselves. Lately, though, Jenny has gotten gentler with the grown-up, not out of respect but out of love. Jenny is finally getting through to the older woman. Today Jenny is going to take this woman through a profound experience, and the woman doesn't know what is about to happen.

Jenny tells her, "I need to introduce you to some people. They really need you to tell them that you think they are OK."

It might be simplest for the storyline for you to know a few things.

1. Jenny was my name until I was 13. My first name is Geneva, so I went by Jenny for short.

2. The older woman in the story is present-day me.

3. The people she wanted me to meet were younger versions of me at different ages of loss.

The first person was me as a 14-month-old baby. This baby's playmate, protector, and biological brother, JJ, had died in a trailer fire. Despite having been given up for adoption at 3 weeks old, her first memory of grief seems to be 14 months old. This baby had a sense that JJ ensured no one forgot her and that he shared his food with her. She crawled up in my lap, and I just held her and rocked her and told her it would be OK until she was ready to sit beside me.

Next was me as a 2-year-old. She was frustrated because she had fallen down a lot while learning to walk, so they nicknamed her Jenny Bump. It felt like they were making fun of her, and she felt like there was something wrong with her. I told her the thing that caused her to fall down was probably the same thing that caused her to get car sick, and I thought she was sweet. I reminded her that Grandma called her Jenny Bump in the sweetest way that made her feel special. I held her until she was ready to sit beside me.

Next was me as an 8-year-old. She had come from her mom's funeral. Despite her Aunt Sheila trying to tell the little girl that she was really her biological mom, the little girl was distraught, lost, and confused. Her dad had left several months earlier. The whispers around the house were that she would be going to Ohio to live with Uncle Jim. She just wanted someone to hold her, comfort her, and remind her that she wouldn't be alone her whole life, so I did.

This went on and on until an 18 –year old came around the corner, and wanted reassurance that she had what it took to survive so far away in the very large city of Fayetteville.

I reassured and hugged each one. They sat in a circle when they were all there and just kept asking over and over again, "Do you love us? Are you proud of us? Have we helped you become who you are? Are you glad you had each of us for the journey of life?" We laughed, and we cried, and I just kept reassuring each of them. They finally settled down and beamed with pride for me.

I had to accept each one of them as a part of me. I could no longer abandon those younger versions of me that still lived inside of me, contributing to the board of directors in my head. I had wanted to ignore them and tell them that they had survived, so I didn't need to acknowledge their pain. After they settled down and I realized that I was truly happy that they had been part of my journey, and I didn't want to leave them abandoned anymore. A weight was lifted from me that I didn't even know I was carrying.

It was more than a year before I could create enough safety in my body to have a similar conversation with my 19-year-old self. Instead of feeling abandoned, she felt judged and ridiculed because her survival tools during her freshman year of college were drinking and random sex. A textbook response to a childhood full of sexual abuse and abandonment. I had spent many years embarrassed by the ways 19-year-old me had coped. When I was on my weight loss journey, I got stuck trying to get to a certain weight. I finally asked myself when was the last time I had been that weight. It was when I was 19. I figured out that the reason I had lied to myself for all those years about being a smaller size was deep down. I was afraid if I got to that size again. I would be a mess like I was when I was 19. Was I conscious of this belief? Heck no. It was only during careful exploration of the root causes of why I was stuck and discovering ways I needed to forgive myself and stop abandoning myself.

I had to go through a similar imaginative process to have a conversation with 19-year-old me. After lots of reassurance, apology, and begging her forgiveness, she finally opened up. She wanted me to also acknowledge all the amazing things she had accomplished. She developed skills as an event planner and volunteer coordinator that have served me so much. She made friendships with people that have lasted 30 years and enriched my life even to this day. She also had tremendous courage to begin therapy. She decided to get healthy before she made a long-term commitment to a spouse. I owe her my very life for the trajectory she set, but I had spent all these years embarrassed and ashamed of her. We came to an understanding. She shared that she was super proud of me and thought my life and my extensive travel were fan-freaking-tastic. I embraced the good with the ugly. I acknowledged how few tools she had and that I was proud of all of her accomplishments. It was profound. Ironically, in the next two weeks, I lost the last five pounds.

Moving through life in a new way takes a degree of care and love for yourself that might be more than you've ever known before –– but you're now well-equipped for the task! And the more you do it, the more you'll see those old patterns shift. The best part? You'll be able to engage with yourself from a place of deep love, and you'll be able to accomplish your goals that much easier because you'll be motivated by that love instead of by fear or criticism.

To sum up:

As you continue to nurture your relationship with yourself, engaging in the process of forgiveness and shedding self-judgment, you will gradually notice a sense of lightness permeating your being. Along this journey, you might also discover that some of the tools you have acquired along the way have proven to be valuable and worth preserving. Just like the lesson of looking both ways before crossing the street, which has served you well in ensuring your safety, you may have learned other tools and skills that still hold significance in your life. Embrace and hold on to those tools that continue to support and benefit you as you navigate your path.

Building this new relationship with yourself will necessitate thoughtful policy reviews. It entails examining various aspects of your identity, exploring different perspectives, and redefining what success means to you personally. Similar to the steps we have taken thus far, we will approach this process one step at a time. It's not about rushing or overwhelming yourself with all the changes at once. Instead, we will gradually and intentionally assess and redefine the policies that shape your self-perception, beliefs, and understanding of success. By approaching this process with patience and taking it step by step, you create a space for growth, self-discovery, and transformation, fostering a healthier and more fulfilling relationship with yourself.

CHAPTER 9
Adopting a new identity

I'm glad you're still here because we're now entering a crucial phase that will equip you with invaluable skills to regulate your emotions throughout your life's journey. You have already learned about the intricacies of your nervous system, the influence of your body on your emotions, and how negative beliefs can take root. You have taken the empowering step of replacing those negative beliefs with positive ones that will support you as you transition from mere survival to flourishing. Furthermore, you have familiarized yourself with the concept of acknowledging and allowing your emotions, and hopefully, you have started implementing this practice in your daily life.

From this point forward, you will continue to practice accepting and understanding your emotions, an exercise that will accompany you for the rest of your life. In this chapter, we will delve deeper into important mindset shifts that will aid you in regulating your nervous system when it inevitably becomes activated instead of hijacking your day, week, month, or year. These mindset shifts will empower you to respond to emotional triggers in a way that maintains your balance and well-being. By embracing these techniques and adopting a mindful approach to emotional regulation, you will develop the resilience and skills necessary to navigate the ups and downs of life with grace and self-awareness.

It all comes down to identity

I want you to know how to go from a person who has been constantly activated, rigid, inflexible, and perhaps lived in a lot of pain to something different, better, and more flexible. : To do this, you must begin to change your self-perception and sense of self. One of the ways to do that is to upgrade your identity and decide what kind of person you want to be. Living life with a calm nervous system is all about intention. Many of us have gone through life just reacting to the things happening and declaring, "This is the way I am, and this is the way it's always been for me." From my perspective, the definition of an ideal life is a well-designed and intentional life. I agree with Socrates, who said an unexamined life is not worth living.

Identity is the bedrock of all the mindset shifts to make . It's your sense of self, the way you talk about yourself to yourself. It's how you see yourself. Your identity also has many facets, including the values you hold dear, how you define who you are, and even physical, psychological, and interpersonal characteristics. As children, our identity is established in our family of origin. Perhaps you were the smart one, the pretty one, the bubbly one, or the shy one.

How you define yourself matters, yet, we often forget that it's up to us. That's one of the reasons I love college students so much: they're in a time of life when it's reasonable and acceptable to be defining who you are. But the truth is, you can do this at any time. You get to decide who you want to be, how you want to be known, and what you stand for. You may have been considered a misfit if you are entrepreneurial in a family of artists. As an adult, you can decide it's OK that your family were artists, and you can still pursue your interests while loving them and allowing them to become accustomed to your identity.

Remember the story of my transition from a recreational biker to a commuting cyclist? When I first started riding my bike for my daily commute, I couldn't believe what the app was telling me. In just five years since my friend's boyfriend convinced me to invest in a good bike, I had pedaled a whopping 120 miles! Feeling the wind in my hair and the joy of cycling, I challenged myself even further. I signed up for a virtual race—a 100-mile journey from Key Largo to Key West. And guess what? I had a max of ten weeks to complete it!

The idea seemed wild at first. Going from a leisurely 120 miles in seven years to a hundred miles in just over seven weeks? Insane, right? But here's the twist: I pushed myself beyond my expectations during those ten incredible weeks. I rode a grand total of 428 miles, averaging 8.25 miles per ride. Can you believe it? What caused this fantastic transformation? It was a shift in my identity—a change in how I saw myself. I stopped seeing myself as a casual cyclist and embraced the belief that I could become a commuter. And that belief propelled me forward, turning my crazy challenge into an exhilarating adventure.

In the last chapter, we delved deeper into your relationship with yourself. Now I want you to think about the ways you've defined yourself. If you were "the shy one," do you still want to be that way? I'm not saying you go from being the shy one to the life of the party or a world-traveling public speaker. However, can you ask yourself, "Is it really true that I'm the shy one?" Many people tell me they are shy until they get to know someone. Then, are you really shy? Or is it possible you are afraid of rejection? Is it possible when you think of walking up to someone you don't know at a networking event or church (places people are expecting to meet new people), your palms sweat, your heart races, and your mind goes blank? You learned earlier that this is simply a nervous system response to perceived danger. What have you made it mean?

Another helpful identity hack is to decide what kind of person you want to be. So, complete the statement, "I'm the kind of person who _____." Hopefully, over time you'll develop a list. Initially, it may not be readily obvious how to fill in the blank. Start with "I'm the kind of person who does hard things." Later you can upgrade to "I do hard things well." When you decide you are the kind of person who does hard things, your whole life gets a bit simpler because this life has plenty of hard things. Your brain likes to be right, so planting this new identity belief allows your brain to help you be right, and it will try hard things.

You can choose many other character traits or ways of being. One mild note of caution, notice if you're defining yourself in ways that inadvertently make life harder than necessary. If your identity is "I'm a hard worker," this can serve you. But what might it look like to upgrade to "Let it be easy?" I recently made this upgrade, and after a lifetime of being a person of perseverance, I have had to see how perseverance can also be used to just sit down and make steady progress on my goal, not just overcome ridiculous obstacles. If I'm constantly looking for huge barriers so I can apply perseverance, I may avoid the simple task of just being consistent.

Another identity hack is to list ways you don't want to be. Then use the list to outline the kind of person you want to be by reframing each one in the positive.

I don't want....	I want to be the kind of person...
to be reactionary	who listens well and responds appropriately
scared all the time of everything	who is courageous
to be constantly triggered	cultivate emotional resiliency
to procrastinate	who keeps their word

Riding in the rain

Even after upgrading my identity to a commuter, I still had all these crazy mental limits about cycling—no riding in the rain or cold for me. Thank you very much! But then something magical happened: I decided to order these awesome windproof pants. Waterproof? Nah, I didn't need those because I wasn't gonna be one of those rain-riding folks. I mean, seriously, as my grandma would say, they didn't have the sense God gave a goose!

One morning, my husband Barry, who noticed how cycling reduces my stress, asked if I was gonna ride to work. I was like, "Nah, too much chance of rain!" But he checked the weather and reminded me we had dinner plans. He even offered to pick me up with the bike rack on the Jeep. Isn't that sweet! His support made me feel confident to ride anywhere, knowing he'd rescue me anytime.

So, I set off before dawn with my fancy new pants on. And wouldn't you know it, the rain started pouring just four miles into my ride. But hey, I thought, I could always call Barry if I needed to. Besides, biking would get me to work faster than waiting for a pickup. I cruised through a well-lit tunnel under the state highway. But the tunnel's exit was unlit, and I rolled right into a massive puddle. I found myself knee-deep in water in a heartbeat, so I quickly unclipped my feet from the pedals (thank goodness it was instinct!) and walked myself back out of the puddle. Soaking wet from the knees down, I stood there pondering my next move. Should I call Barry? But no! I told myself, "Okay, just walk out of this tunnel and then assess the rain situation." And so, I did just that. I crossed the state highway, thankful that traffic was light at that hour. The rain was now more of a sprinkle, so I pedaled onward. Lo and behold, I discovered that the return vent at work dried my pants like a champ by day's end.

Despite the pouring rain, I was determined to try riding back home. My co-workers were alarmed. "It's pouring, for goodness sake!" they admonished. But hey, I had spent a whopping $45 on those pants, and I wanted to put them to the ultimate test. One of my colleagues scoffed, saying, "$45 isn't much, and honestly, I don't care if you spent $100 — it's still pouring!" We all had a good laugh, and I gave Barry a call before embarking on my watery adventure.

I was willing to push my limits, but I also had a healthy respect for them. Maneuvering around puddles on the trail was getting trickier, especially since the trail was nestled close to several creeks. How had I never noticed them before? With the water rising, those creeks seemed way too close for comfort. I stopped along the way and called Barry, admitting that maybe, just maybe, I might not make it. But that sweet man assured me he was keeping an eye on my progress via our location app and would happily come to pick me up. When he finally pulled up under an awning to load my bike, I couldn't help but chuckle at his attempt to stay dry when I was drenched head to toe. Instead of our usual routine of him loading the bike while I changed shoes, I insisted he stayed dry this time.

Your identity is the basis of any new habits you want to incorporate. In Atomic Habits, James Clear says that when you change your identity, and adopt new habits, you are casting a vote for the person you are trying to become. I didn't begin being someone who could ride to work, much less someone who could ride in the cold, dark, or rain. But each day I got on my bike and rode 1 mile, then another, I cast a vote to the identity I'm a biking commuter.

When you change your identity, you change everything –your possibilities, future self, and responses. Sometimes when you are changing your identity, you don't even know how it will serve you later.

Shifting perspective

Remember how we talked about how the collection of beliefs shapes your worldview, also known as your perspective? The extent to which you can regulate your nervous system is heavily influenced by your perspective. Perspective refers to how you perceive and interpret things and is shaped by the accumulation of various experiences and beliefs. While we have made significant progress in addressing negative influences, there may still be survival strategies from the past that need upgrading. Recognizing that perspective is a choice to facilitate this upgrading process is crucial.

However, many people tend to rely on their initial automatic thoughts, leaving their perspective susceptible to the influence of unresolved childhood issues. Without realizing it, you may find yourself overwhelmed by a flood of sensations and unexamined thoughts.

Since a significant portion of your perspective was formed during childhood, it may be necessary to reevaluate how you have viewed the world. It's necessary to upgrade your filters so that things that were once perceived as threats can now be categorized as minor annoyances or may not even register as noteworthy.

For instance, if you developed a perspective in childhood that led you to believe that everyone will inevitably abandon you, your coping mechanism might have been to avoid getting close to anyone. Alternatively, if someone does not respond to your text quickly enough, you might interpret it as them leaving you, just like others did in the past.

During this period of change, it's a fantastic opportunity to reevaluate the deeply entrenched beliefs and assumptions you've held onto and determine if they continue to benefit you. It's like the policy review I mentioned when an organization gets new leadership. Adult You is the leader, and everything you've learned up to now needs review.

Remember the wisdom imparted by our parents?

Don't talk to strangers.

Don't touch hot stoves.

Don't associate with the wrong crowd.

Don't stand out.

Don't cry, or else I'll give you something to cry about

Quit asking for things.

As an adult, you now have the power to consciously assess whether these directives align with your aspirations for the life you desire. You don't necessarily have to discard every aspect of your perspective. For instance, the principles of looking both ways before crossing the street and avoiding hot stoves are still valuable coping mechanisms that ensure your safety. These perspectives continue to serve you, so feel free to retain them.

What and how vs. why

When we encounter the need to shift our perspective, we often find ourselves tempted to ask the question, "Why am I like this?" We believe that if we can recall the specific time or event that shaped our perspective, we can somehow find a clue to fixing it. However, I have discovered that it can be more helpful to inquire, "When is the first time you remember feeling this way?"

Sometimes, when we approach our sensations and ask if they have a message for us, a memory can suddenly emerge in our minds. It is unnecessary to pinpoint the exact moment when the perspective was formed; what matters is allowing the sensations to surface and releasing them. By acknowledging and releasing these sensations, we create space for new perspectives to emerge.

After allowing the sensations to subside (don't skip this step), a more effective question to ask ourselves is, "What do I want my response to be?" or "How do I want to handle similar situations in the future?" Instead of dwelling on the past and searching for explanations, we shift our focus toward our desired responses and actions. This forward-thinking approach empowers us to consciously choose how we want to navigate similar circumstances, fostering personal growth and positive change.

Reframing perspective: "Every ride is a water ride at Worlds of Fun!"

When Sami was in fourth grade, she was all fired up and ready to conquer the world as a Junior Scout and me as her Scout leader. The scout council gave us some advice, saying that the Juniors should take charge and be the masters of their troop. And boy, did I take that to heart! Maybe a tad too much for my fellow co-leaders liking.

So, when it was time to sell those delicious cookies, we put our heads together and brainstormed. The girls had this grand idea to use the cookie money for a trip to Kansas City, a place with an amazing amusement park called Worlds of Fun. Naturally, they had to sell the cookies first, so I let them take the reins on everything. They got to organize the cookie orders, decide how many extra to snag for selling at booths, count the cash, and understand the whole shebang. And when it came to planning the trip, my co-leader had serious doubts that I'd follow through with the Worlds of Fun adventure. But why the heck not? They met their goal and then some! Selling those cookies was a piece of cake for those awesome older girls because they had a clear goal in mind: We're gonna rock Worlds of Fun!

Now, here's a fun fact about me: I'm not exactly the camping type. So, my Girl Scout troop wasn't exactly the camping type either. Back then, roughing it for me meant staying at a motel with an outdoor pool. But you know what? My incredible girls had the chance to plan their own trip, and instead of pitching tents, we hit the mall to learn the art of shopping. They got a real-world education on how much things cost and how to budget like pros, even if starting a fire wasn't their strong suit.

As luck would have it, when we finally arrived in Kansas City, the rain gods decided to play a prank on us. Talk about a bummer, right? But did we let a little rain ruin our spirits? No way! We decided to check into the hotel and hoped the rain would give up its game. To pass the time, I braided all the girls' hair, and we even managed to find a store that sold ponchos. And so, armed with our ponchos, we charged ahead to the amusement park in the rain—no lightning, of course. You won't believe it, but my fellow leaders thought I had lost my marbles with this idea. Even a few of the girls were a tad nervous. So, I turned to them and asked, "Hey, what's the best part of an amusement park?" They all shouted, "The water rides!" And that's when I dropped the bomb: "Well, guess what? In the rain, every ride's a water ride!" Their faces lit up, and off we went!

We braved a few rides in the rain, and you know what happened next? The rain finally stopped! It was like a miracle! And guess what? We practically had the whole darn park to ourselves for the first two hours. No waiting in lines, no sweating like mad—just pure, glorious fun!

Since that epic adventure, my family and I have lived by a special code: "Every ride is a water ride." It's our way of saying, "Let's make the best of any situation, no matter what." It's been a total game-changer, a perspective shift of seismic proportions. Have you ever had a moment like this? A moment when life pushed you to see things from a whole new angle? And hey, maybe you could use that experience as a launching pad for other mind-blowing shifts in perspective. The possibilities are endless!

Reset your body as well as your mind

In our journey of living with a less activated nervous system, I've shared how we need to notice what's happening in our body and be aware of our body's reactions to thoughts and feelings. This can be easier said than done, though, especially if you're used to being disconnected from your body.

That's why it's important to practice body-awareness techniques like yoga. According to Bessel van der Kolk, yoga may improve the functioning of traumatized individuals by helping them allow physical and sensory experiences associated with fear and helplessness, increase emotional awareness, and affect tolerance. This is just a fancy way to say that it gives you a safe place to allow your body to experience all the sensations. Learning to control your body in a yoga environment provides practice the next time you notice your heart racing, your palms sweating, and other unpleasant sensations.

I highly recommend it because it's also such a great metaphor for life. As you start yoga, you show up on the mat and check in with yourself. How are you showing up at this moment? You set an intention for the class or practice. Do you want to add peace, serenity, gentleness, or love? Next, you settle in and begin to take long slow breaths and really pay attention to your breath. While it may seem impossible to take this outside the yoga classroom, when you are at a meeting, what would change if you sat in your chair for a moment and asked yourself, "How am I showing up today?" Could you take a long slow breath while the meeting is getting underway? How would that change your ability to respond during the meeting or encounter?

As you begin to stretch, you receive instruction to notice where there's tension and ask your body if it's ready to release the tension. Gentle slow movement accomplishes the goal of increasing flexibility. See, there's that word, flexibility. At the beginning of yoga, you may be rigid and tight, but you will likely be more flexible after stretching and breathing. Just like when you begin the process of tuning into your body, you may not know how to do it and feel rigid and clumsy, but with practice, you will become more flexible.

In yoga, there's no winner or loser. There's no competition. It's simply a way to tune into your body and move it to give you a greater ability to release tension and provide the tools to journey through life more in touch with your body.

The primary lesson I've learned from yoga is how to accept yourself. The resistance you feel as you attempt a new pose often represents the resistance you're feeling in your life. Or it can be if you are aware. When I can be gentler with myself on the yoga mat, I can be gentler with myself outside the yoga space. I can learn to be easy when I lack flexibility. I can also use the flexibility I learn on the mat to bring to the rest of the world, changing how I show up in those spaces. For instance, I hate downward dog. I don't know how people see it as a resting pose. My arms quiver, my shoulders lock up, and I feel weak, which frustrates me. Then if I look at my life and when I choose to rest, how does that make me feel? At the moment, I feel like it is good. But at the end of a long weekend of rest, I often start beating myself up for all the things I didn't do. The things I didn't accomplish. Do I celebrate that I accomplished the task of resting? Nope.

Similar to the experience of finding a counselor, not all yoga centers are created equally. When we decided to start yoga, someone suggested we utilize the fact that every yoga center typically offers a discounted first-month membership. It can feel a bit like Goldilocks. This one was too hard. This one too easy. This one is just right. At the first studio we tried, it seemed everyone was the age of our 20-something children. The instructors would tell you the next pose to take and then say, "If you can't do that, here's the easier pose." The yoga center we settled on gave everyone the easy pose first. They would say, "If it's in your practice or if you want to challenge yourself, you can also do it," and they would give a more difficult version of the pose. It felt unifying. I noticed that the folks around me that were regulars often had a few more lines around their eyes than me. When they did the harder poses, it was inspiring. It felt like they had done the work to increase their flexibility. There was a strength that came from practice. That's not to say that there weren't young people in the studio, just it wasn't who my eye was drawn to.

In 2018, I received a very cool invitation for a paid speaking gig at a New Teacher Orientation in Missouri. Now, I couldn't just dash off to this town without knowing a thing or two about it. So, my adventurous spirit and I talked my husband into turning it into a fabulous weekend getaway. Little did we know that our quest for knowledge would lead us on a surprising yoga adventure!

Now, let me be clear, we weren't exactly yoga masters. But hey, we loved to dabble in the art of yoga whenever we had the chance. We considered ourselves wandering explorers, always ready to unroll our yoga mats wherever we ended up. In fact, we were so prepared for spontaneous escapades that we had a stash of hammocks and beach towels stowed away in our trusty Jeep, ready to be deployed at a moment's notice for our weekend adventures.

Our journey to Missouri began with an enchanting discovery -- a community yoga class right smack in the heart of the town. And guess what? It was scheduled for Saturday morning, the perfect way to kick start our weekend of exploration. This wasn't just any ordinary yoga class, though. This one was set up in a park just a hop, skip, and a jump away from the bustling farmer's market. Talk about combining healthy vibes with fresh produce!

The very experienced instructor made yoga more approachable than anything I had experienced up to that point. She promoted focusing on being gentle with ourselves and our practice. "Hey, friends, check in with your knee! How's it feeling in this pose?" she would kindly remind us. Wait, what? My knee? My knee wasn't even involved in this pose! But, curious as we were, we decided to go along with it. And you know what? It turned out to be a revelation! Checking in with our knees, ankles, necks, and every other body part she mentioned brought a whole new level of awareness to our practice.

By the end of that relaxing morning, we realized that yoga wasn't just about bending and twisting our bodies into pretzel-like shapes. It was about connecting with ourselves, honoring our bodies, and embracing the gentle peace that lay within. That wonderful instructor not only taught us yoga but also imparted a valuable life lesson: to be kind to ourselves and approach everything we do with a sense of gentleness and curiosity. And so, armed with newfound wisdom and a refreshed spirit, we continued our weekend adventure in Missouri, ready to embrace whatever surprises and delights the town had in store for us. But one thing was certain: our yoga practice would never be the same again.

As we've discussed, fight-or-flight as a default operating mode wreaks havoc on your body. Yoga gives you concentrated time to give your body the safe message to return to homeostasis. I love that it's called a yoga practice because it's not one-and-done. Consider adding it to your toolkit of ways to live with a regulated nervous system.

Intentionally send the all-clear

The final step in working toward regulating your nervous system is to intentionally send the message to your body that it is safe. If you watch an antelope outrun a lion, the antelope shake it off after escaping. It releases all the fight-or-flight chemicals and helps the antelope return to homeostasis. You are getting danger messages all day long. People cut you off in traffic, arguments with spouses, you know, life. You have to find a release. For you, it could be to sing your favorite song at the top of your lungs or scream in the car on the way home, it could be to go for a run, jump on an indoor trampoline, or it could be to have a dance party in your living room.

Dancing takes flexibility and immersion in the music. It turns out that the less you care about what other people think, the more you can hear and feel the music and respond accordingly. It's like the fear of others watching you actually makes you more rigid and worse at dancing. Also, uninhibited dancing releases and changes energy, which for me, generates amazing joy.

Even if you have teenagers that roll their eyes at you, who cares. If dancing in the living room means you don't take out the day's stress on them, they will come to appreciate it. If you aren't into dancing, consider what else you can do to add play, fun, and laughter to your life. Laughter is good medicine because it releases yummy brain chemicals critical for regulating your nervous system.

Redefining success

Previously, when I encountered negative beliefs, I set goals to prove they weren't true. Hit a certain revenue number in business to prove I am enough. Run a 5K every month to prove I have what it takes. As I've cleaned out my toxic waste barrels of negative beliefs, I struggled for a while to figure out the motivation for setting goals. What I've discovered is that I am now setting goals as experiments to figure out what I like and don't like. I had set a revenue goal in our business to prove I had what it takes. I worked really hard the year I accomplished the goal. I didn't have a good work-life/balance, was completely stressed out, and didn't enjoy my life. Now I've set the same goal with a change in variables. I want to work diligently, giving my clients great value. I want to be able to enjoy my family, and I want sufficient time to travel without working. I want to see if I like the variables and enjoy my life. It's a lot less about striving and surviving and more about growing and evolving as a person. Wouldn't it be great to live a smooth, peaceful life? Maybe. It might also be boring. I'll let you know if I ever get there.

Success is not constant ease. Success is overcoming things and then celebrating. Brooke Castillo teaches the concept that life is 50/50. Jesus taught the concept, "In this world, you'll have you will have trouble." Between those important teachers in my life, I have accepted living with a calm nervous system does not mean you are without any activation. It means you learn to experience the sensations that come up and then allow them to naturally return to homeostasis.

While pursuing a master's degree in Internet marketing, one of my classes required me to create a 15-20 minute video. The task involved multiple steps: writing the script, filming the video, and editing it. The primary objective was to gain proficiency in video editing software and learn effective video shooting techniques. Initially, the process was quite time-consuming, and my first video took me around 15 or 16 hours to complete. I found myself thinking, "I don't have this kind of time," which is similar to what many people express when it comes to processing their emotions.

However, I persisted and tackled the assignment again the following week. As I continued to practice, my time investment gradually decreased. The second video took me 13 hours, and the week after that, I managed to finish in 11 hours. Over the span of a year, consistently working on these video projects, I honed my skills. By the time I reached the last class, which required creating a 15-minute video podcast, I was able to write the script, shoot the footage, and edit it in less than two hours. It was a significant transformation. But I had to be willing to invest the time to be bad to get good.

I bet if you think of anything you are now good at, you likely weren't good at it the first time. As you go through this process of learning how to emotionally regulate your nervous system, I hope you will have a student approach and always be learning. I often say we arrive in the coffin; until then it's a journey.

To sum up:

As you delve into the realm of emotional regulation and acquire its tools, you will witness a continuous improvement in your ability to navigate life with greater flexibility and lightness. Understanding that this doesn't imply a complete avoidance of adversity is essential. As long as you're alive and breathing, obstacles are bound to come your way. However, as we develop and practice these emotional regulation tools, just like my journey with video editing software, we enhance our capacity to maneuver through these challenges successfully.

Our goal is not to have a completely flat lined nervous system devoid of any emotional fluctuations. Rather, our aim is to embrace the natural ebb and flow of life. This entails allowing things to happen that may upset or excite us and granting our bodies the opportunity to complete the emotional cycle and return to a state of balance, known as homeostasis. It's about acknowledging the inevitable ups and downs, giving ourselves permission to experience the full spectrum of emotions, and finding effective ways to swiftly regain our flow after a temporary disruption.

In the upcoming chapter, we will explore strategies on how to deal with individuals in your life who might seem determined to ruin your good mood. Additionally, we will discuss how you can regain control of your emotional regulation, acting as the master of your own emotional remote control. By implementing these techniques, you will gain valuable insights into managing challenging social dynamics and reclaiming authority over your emotional well-being.

CHAPTER 10
Relationships – source of joy and frustration

Welcome to the next to the last chapter, where we embark on a journey to explore the art of navigating challenging interactions with others and regaining control over our emotional well-being. Life often presents us with individuals who seem determined to disrupt our positive mood and inner balance. However, it is within our power to reclaim the remote control of our emotional regulation and respond to such situations with grace and resilience. In this chapter, we will delve into practical strategies and insights that will empower you to handle these encounters effectively and maintain your emotional equilibrium.

Throughout our lives, we encounter various personalities and dynamics that can impact our emotions and overall well-being. Whether it's a difficult colleague, a demanding family member, or a critical friend, their actions and words can leave us feeling overwhelmed and unsettled. But fret not, for this chapter is dedicated to equipping you with the tools and techniques necessary to navigate these challenging relationships with confidence and composure.

By understanding the underlying dynamics at play and implementing strategies tailored to each situation, you will discover the power to regain control over your emotional responses. You will learn how to shield yourself from negativity, establish healthy boundaries, and communicate assertively to protect your own emotional well-being. So, let's embark on this empowering journey together as we unlock the secrets to managing difficult interactions and taking back control of our emotional remote control.

Relationships

Sitting with yourself in your happy, quiet place, you can maintain your nervous system regulation pretty well. I love the prayer that says, "Lord, so far today, I haven't done any of the things you say I shouldn't do, but in a moment, I'm going to get out of bed, and then I'm going to need your help." Unless you are a hermit, you will experience things that activate your nervous system. You are human, it means your body is functioning properly, and it ensures you will survive.

Most of us are not content with just survival. We yearn to lead meaningful lives free from being overwhelmed by difficult emotions and stress. Unfortunately, the people, places, and things around us can make an already out-of-control emotional state worse. Being able to live with a regulated nervous system seems like an unrealistic dream for many. You may recognize some of the triggers I deal with, such as loud noise, excess clutter, or harrowing physical situations –– like after almost drowning at the beach or feeling anxious in tight spaces. Beyond my own personal experience, the fear associated with work events —such as employee evaluations, demands for sales, confrontation, or intense job interviews— is something practically all of us can relate to.

On top of these undoubtedly unsettling situations is negotiating relationships with spouses and family members, either explicitly in a statement or the looks or sounds they make to indicate you aren't on the same page. Not to mention, because my body keeps score, I've noticed how at certain times of the year, I'm a bit more sensitive. When I dig into why, I realize that traumatic things may have happened during this time of year, like the anniversary of deaths or birthdays of loved ones who have passed.

During this season of learning to feel, you may have to limit the people who activate you. Having someone tell you the truth about your blind spot is different than subjecting yourself to someone who refuses to be careful with your heart and your healing journey. I have told Barry being in relationship is like someone asking me to play soccer, I can share with them that I'd love to, as long as they know I'm still recovering from a hurt ankle. Someone who wants a relationship agrees to be careful with your injury. They are humans and will still make mistakes, but the attempt is there. If somone refuses to be careful, it may be time to take a break from the relationships.

Let's go over a few things to remember in these situations that may help you deactivate yourself. In some situations, having a friend or family member assist you may be helpful, which is called co-regulating. If the person is the one who activated you, to begin with, be aware that it may be difficult for them to set aside their own nervous system response to be able to assist you.

That makes sense

A first and crucial step when trying to understand your own or others' nervous systems is validating the feelings behind them. It doesn't mean you have to agree with the thoughts running through their mind. Often, just acknowledging their concerns can provide comfort. As we discussed in the chapter on creating emotional safety for yourself, all it takes is a simple phrase like, "Of course, that makes sense," to create a secure space where our loved one can engage with their emotions. When you validate the underlying feeling, you let your loved ones know they are seen and heard, and you aren't going to whip out your critical voice on them. With this, you are well on your way to living more engaged, well-designed lives!

I have a friend who is married to an engineer. They went to marriage therapy, and one of the best takeaways was for the therapist to teach her husband to say, "That makes sense." He fought it really hard at first because it didn't make sense in his mind. She would say, "I feel like I'm not a priority to you when I tell you what the plan is, and then one hour later, you ask me what the plan is again. It feels like you don't listen to me, and if you prioritized me, you would listen."

He would want to tell her all the ways he makes her a priority, and this tiny example (in his mind) doesn't prove that he doesn't prioritize her. The therapist explained that our feelings often don't actually make sense to us or anyone else. You've probably heard that fear is often completely irrational. But our feelings feel very real, and they are trying to tell us something.

The therapist had to explain to the engineer husband that in his head, he could add things like "from your perspective," "from your life experience," or whatever else to help him understand her point of view. He may not know that she repeatedly told her mom she wanted her to come to school and have lunch with her sometime, but the mom was too busy working. This made her feel like she wasn't a priority to her mom. So my friend's amygdala scans this incident with her husband, it matches an existing glitchy file labeled not a priority, so it sends sensations flooding her body to warn of potential danger. When she tells him this story, then he can say, "Oh, that actually does make sense." Often, we don't know the origin of the feeling of unsafety; we can just identify the pain or discomfort we feel. If he can say, "That makes sense that if I don't listen to what you say, you feel like you aren't a priority." Then ready for the magic? He can follow up with, "Is there anything I can do to make you feel like a priority?"

In another case, she may say, "I just want you to sit with me because I'm overwhelmed by the dirty house, and the dirty dishes and you are leaving town." His response is vital. He's a doer who loves to show love with acts of service. He can sit on the couch and hold her for a while, or he can jump up and clean the house and the dishes. When he cleans the house and the dishes, he thinks he's helping alleviate the overwhelm, which he thinks will translate into proving he prioritizes her. She may sit on the couch feeling very alone and feel very sad. Another fight is likely brewing. Being sad doesn't feel safe, so she will likely respond angrily to his attempts to wash the dishes unless he sits with her as she had asked.

The terrible thing is that most of us don't know how to ask someone to sit with us. We think cleaning the dishes will help. Then we say things like, "Too little, too late," because we are bewildered that working on the dishes isn't helping us feel better.

It's possible that this is triggering one of those mis-wirings from childhood that you aren't lovable or not valuable. Here's the really dumb thing. We don't realize we are sad because our person didn't sit with us. And we don't know what to do with the flood of sensations. So let's talk through a couple of things you need to understand about these sensations.

Two key things to know about emotions:

Remember, emotions are indicator lights, not an indictment.

Emotions are like headlights when you are lost in the dark. Their purpose is not to condemn us for our chosen road but to help us recognize and understand which path we should take. They can guide us through life's journey positively and joyfully. It's a reminder that even in uncertain times, we always have emotions to give us direction. Our emotions can act as beacons of hope, helping us keep focused on the big picture even when things appear dire or uncertain. Just remember: emotions are indicators — seek them out and let them provide illumination into life's unknown roads!

Emotions are real, but may not be true

It's true that emotions can be so very real, almost like a tangible thing we can put our finger on. But what those emotions teach us is they may not always reflect the reality of the situation. While our emotions are important and should not be ignored. It may be wise to step back and survey life more objectively to gain insight and knowledge to better understand of any given moment in time. After all, with understanding comes power and hopefully peace amongst the turmoil of the nervous system response. If you can begin to take on the observer role instead of judge, you'll be able to just notice what's happening and ask yourself questions. I hope you don't fall into the trap I sometimes do of saying, I should be over this by now, or I should feel different. That would be nice, but your emotions are telling you something still needs processing or healing. Adding should will just keep you stuck.

One word of caution. You've learned an awful lot up to this point about emotions and feelings. Please do not use this information against the people you are in a relationship with, especially not out loud. I can hear it now, the engineer husband says, "You don't feel like you are a priority because of a mixed-up wiring from your mom's dysfunction and lack of priority. And another thing, your thoughts create your feelings, so if you are feeling this way, it's because of what you are thinking, so you should maybe choose not to think of me in this way. See, it's not my fault you don't feel like you are a priority." It makes me want to include a release of liability from the engineer's wife when she smothers him in his sleep.

Trust me for all the times I've messed it up. Just listen and hear the person. If you need to respond (because sometimes you may need to sit quietly), try saying, "Of course, honey, that makes sense. What do you need from me right now?" If you can't say that with sincerity, then you might try, "Wow, that sounds really hard." Remember, you may not have the whole story, and from their perspective, it might be really hard with their skills and abilities. As you complete your own emotional cycles, you'll be less activated by the people around you and be able to stay open, curious, and compassionate.

Assume positive intent

The next step in de-escalating your nervous system response, especially dealing with people, is to assume positive intent. Your children aren't trying to upset you by leaving their shoes on the floor and playing too loud. Your co-worker's insensitive email reply may have come because they were having a really hard day and didn't realize how it would come across. If your husband's comment could be taken two ways, assuming he meant it better is to your advantage. This is not to say ignore abuse or discount your emotions. It's just that sometimes we may need to stop and say out loud, "Did you mean to make it sound like I don't do anything around the house?" By assuming positive intent, then stopping to ask for clarification, you reduce the fuel in the furnace of your nervous system.

After investing in a really nice bike with clips, I fully embraced being a biker. When I travel, I love to use bikes as transportation. I've rented bikes in San Francisco, Milwaukee, Miami, London, Jersey in the Channel Islands, and Washington, DC, which used to be my favorite place because of all the protected bike lanes. After my healing journey, I find that Rome's cobblestone streets and everyone sharing the road together with kindness is my new favorite biking experience.

San Francisco proved particularly interesting because Barry and I rented bikes after I had been seriously biking for a year. All that biking down Mt Comfort Road in Fayetteville, a rural five-lane road with bike lanes where the drivers aren't necessarily thinking about sharing the road, had really built my confidence. The upside of this confidence came on busy streets in San Francisco without a protected bike lane. My nerves stayed relatively calm.

The challenge came in believing Google Maps' assertion about a "mostly flat" section. It's San Francisco. Mostly flat is very relative. I had adapted to using my clipped-in status to be able to get extra velocity from pushing down and pulling up. Not the case when wearing Teva sandals (my second favorite footwear for biking). Additionally, I underestimated how much I used changing gears to give me the power I needed. The difference between four speeds and 14 speeds becomes monumental when it comes to maneuvering up hills. The final element causing a challenge came from realizing that, as a commuter, I only thought of my own safety. Barry has far fewer miles of experience (like about a third of mine). He also wore jeans that day, and constantly worried about how much farther we had to go. So Barry kept pulling his phone from his pocket at every stop light and trying to put it back in when the light turned green. I expressed my concern tersely about him weaving all over the place every time he tried to put the phone back in his pocket. To accommodate my worry, he began trying to ride much faster than me to get to the next stoplight so he could check the phone and put it back in his pocket without weaving. For me, this eliminated the joy of riding together.

For all these reasons, biking from our hotel to Golden Gate Park, a mostly flat, three-mile journey, caused me to be a raving lunatic by the end. I commented early in the trip about how great it is to feel so confident at something physical and to feel like I could be helpful to Barry. I would ride behind him so that I could be a bit defensive with traffic and also have a stronger ability to get out of the way of traffic. It seemed to me after I told Barry I felt strong and confident, he made it a point to leave me behind on every block. I told myself terrible stories, including things like, "He just can't handle me being better at something than him" or "He hates that I'm stronger than him in this one area."

I became livid, and those stories made me madder by the minute. Finally, I found a bike rack and returned my bike. I offered to let him keep riding since he didn't want to ride with me anyway. After absolutely losing my mind and screaming at him in the street, I tried to drink some water and calm myself down.

As I talked about in Chapter three, many of us have experienced abandonment that creates many incomplete emotional loops. Our brains are predicting machines, on constant alert for danger. My brain attempted to convince me Barry wanted to leave me. Additionally, we'd planned this trip as a reward and respite from the harrowing experience of being publicly fired from the housing authority two months earlier, and it also started a few days before my birthday, a time of year fraught with previous trauma from attending my mom's funeral on my eighth birthday.

For most of our marriage, when I got like this, Barry just gave me space to calm down, and from my perspective, this meant we swept it under the rug and filed it as my issue. After we had walked a couple of blocks and I had calmed way down, Barry did something I had been begging him to do for years. He got curious about why he acted the way he did. From his point of view, he had never given a thought about me being stronger than him. He's actually very proud of how far I've come in my ability to ride and overcome obstacles. He expressed his goal of not making me a nervous wreck with the phone. He reasoned in his mind, "If I get to the light really fast, I can check my phone and get it back in my pocket before the light turns so I can make Angela more comfortable while still getting to check my phone." When he explained this, I asked, "Why did you need to check your phone when the map said to go 17 blocks? Couldn't you just remember the street name or count the blocks?" He hadn't considered this logic, and it was entertaining to watch his face as his brain acted like a computer that had frozen up because of too many tabs open. I at least had the reassurance that he wasn't trying to make me feel bad or less than.

For me, it reminded me to assume positive intent. It also gave me a very visceral reminder of how my thoughts can create some crazy feelings. Which actually leads to another step in the journey to calming your nervous system. While I believe that emotions are indicators that our body needs our attention, our feelings are a direct result of our thoughts, which means that it's important to...

Notice your thought habits

If your husband or child cooks a meal for you which is out of the norm and then leaves a big mess in the kitchen, you can think of at least two possible thoughts, "Why do they leave this big mess for me to clean up?" or "How nice that they spent time on a weeknight cooking dinner. I really appreciate their efforts."

Notice when something tweaks your danger sensor, kind of like when the antelope pops its head up and flicks its ears. This is the emotion. Notice all the potential thoughts that come up as a result of the danger sensor. My thoughts during that bike ride were:
Barry wants to leave me.

He can't stand it that I'm better at something than him.

Why doesn't he want to be with me?

What kind of feelings do you think those thoughts created? Anger, upset, misery, all kinds of things. When I stopped to ask him why he did it, and let his nervous system calm down so he could explore what he'd been thinking, none of our thoughts lined up. He reiterated that he's so proud of how much I've accomplished on the bike. His primary thought was actually trying to keep me calm.

While noticing thought habits, you may notice that you sometimes catastrophize things or just assume the worst will happen. It is not helpful unless your goal is only survival and not thriving in a well-designed life.

I've found that mantras are helpful in overcoming a nasty thought habit. So if you've lived in an activated state, you may say, "I'm OK. I'm safe." When hard times come up, I say, "This too shall pass." Personally, I'm not apt to say this when things are going well, but it's actually just as true. Similarly, if you are afraid of losing your job or a relationship, you can say, "If I lose my job, I will figure it out."

Other people will do things differently than you

In the last chapter, we learned about changing our perspective, but what about how that affects relationships? Let's see how our perspectives can be compared to sunglasses and headphones. Picture this: When it's feeling a bit stuck, your nervous system starts making a checklist of things it considers dangerous. As we've learned—everyone's checklist is unique because we all have different experiences, different perspectives.

Now, imagine you're about to tie the knot and walk down the aisle. Before you do, I want you to think of your life experiences as layers of tinted sunglasses or the stations your headphones are tuned into. You know those Bluetooth earphones can only receive what they're tuned into. And guess what? Your device, your brain, has been jamming to a specific set of playlists since you were a little kid. But hold up, your partner has been rocking to a different beat, different playlists altogether.

Think of those wireless headphones as a filter that takes everything in the world and translates it through the lens of your experiences. And here's the kicker—your filter is totally different from other people's filters. It's like wearing sunglasses with scratches and a cool blue tint. Your vision of the world is gonna be a whole different trip, man. But as you learn to live with a calmer nervous system, you'll start noticing that your headphones' frequency and your sunglasses' vision are changing. Not only does it look different to you, but even in your everyday interactions, you'll notice that other people's frequencies are totally groovy and different from yours.

When our kids were little, my friend and her husband embarked on a fabulous Florida trip. Meanwhile, we had this brilliant idea to rendezvous with them in Charlotte, NC, for the NASCAR All-Star race on their way back home. With tickets priced at a mere $10 each and seven kids between us who adored NASCAR, it was a plan made in racing heaven. We took our sweet time driving to Charlotte, making a pit stop in Nashville, where we wandered around a Parthenon replica like adventurous explorers.

Let me tell you, NASCAR events attract all kinds of people. You've got high-flying executives sitting next to folks who could pass as extras from "The Beverly Hillbillies" and everything in between. The format of the All-Star race allows your senses to adapt to the mind-bogglingly loud noise. Surprisingly, with the cars zooming around the track, there are only 20 laps, then a break, then another 20 laps, and so on. Thank goodness I was prepared for the deafening roar of those powerful engines, or my first race experience might have blown out my eardrums!

But here's where things got interesting. On the ride back home, we discovered that not everyone road trips like we do. On the way to Charlotte, our intention was simple: enjoy the journey. But on the way back, efficiency and speed took center stage. Our road trip rules dictated that stops were limited to absolute necessities, with everyone taking care of their biological needs. When we stopped, it was like a synchronized dance — everyone peed, got back in the car, and prepared to hit the road. Barry took the first shift at the gas pump, and if the kids were old enough, whoever finished first would take over so Barry could use the restroom. If the kids were too young, which was the case until our oldest turned 12, Barry finished pumping gas, and by the time I had wrangled everyone back into their car seats, he would be done with his bathroom break. The whole process usually took us around 11 to 15 minutes unless we needed a meal.

Now, our friends had a completely different strategy. They believed in stopping only when the car was running on fumes. If their boys needed to pee, they'd whip out an empty Coke bottle (ugh, that smell!), and as for the girls, they simply restricted their fluid intake to avoid misery. So, when they stopped at our regular intervals of every three hours or so, their kids hadn't even stirred from their seats and hadn't bothered with putting on shoes. I swear, by the time my kids finished their bathroom break and got back in the car, their youngest was just crawling out of the backseat, casually saying, "I don't have to pee." Talk about frustrating!

From our perspective, our way was right, and theirs was wrong. And you know what? From my friend's husband's point of view, we stopped way too often, causing all the trouble. Ironically, as the years went by, I started asking people about their road trip habits, and it's been fascinating. We have other friends who would never eat in the car. They prefer to sit down at a restaurant and enjoy a meal. Can you believe it? Here's the kicker, though — none of these ways are wrong. They're just different. You'll encounter various ways of journeying through life when you navigate friendships or relationships. Some folks want to talk endlessly about past hurts, while others prefer to avoid any kind of heavy conversation. Neither approach is wrong or right. Life would be filled with frustration if we couldn't acknowledge and respect these differences and find a way that serves both parties.

My value was all about not being miserable. If I needed to pee or get a bite to eat, you bet I'd make a stop. On the other hand, my friend was all about efficiency. He wanted to reach home and rest as soon as possible. Neither perspective is wrong; they're just different. By being conscious of your own perspective, you can choose which playlist you allow to play through the headphones of your experience.

If that doesn't work, reparent yourself

I have discovered another technique that seems odd but may be helpful to you. In my mind (sometimes out loud), I notice myself whining like crazy, "I'm hungry," "I'm cold," or "I'm bored." I'll try to explore if this is an indicator light of something going on. I'll sit with myself and ask what I need. Then sometimes, I get tired of listening to myself whine when there's nothing really wrong, or I don't actually need something. So I'll say in my stern parent voice, "OK, so you are hungry, you just ate X minutes ago, you plan to eat again in a little while, and sometimes you will be hungry. So what? Big deal, you're hungry, you aren't going to die." If I'm cold,

I'll have to say, "Well, you don't have a coat. You can't do anything about it, and you are making yourself miserable. You aren't going to die, big deal."

I don't recommend this as a first step in the process, but after trying this a few times, I've found it's helpful to just quiet the whiny voice in certain situations. It's like asking that board member to sit down for a while and take a break from pointing out everything wrong.

Humans saying sentences

Let me share one more tidbit about embracing the journey even when other people seem determined to drive you bonkers. I know you've been there: you're trying every trick in the book to stay calm and positive. You're thinking good thoughts, assuming positive intent, taking deep breaths — heck, you're trying everything! But no matter what, it feels like the universe is out to make you angry. Been there, my friend. Been there.

Recently, something similar happened to me. I asked my youngest not to finish the puzzle that I had started. Might seem weird unless you know, she's a puzzle whiz and often takes charge when we work on one together. Normally, it's her puzzle, so she has every right to do so. But this time, it was my puzzle, a gift just for me. While I appreciate her help, I wanted the satisfaction of completing my gift. So, I mentioned it again later in the day, not remembering that I had already brought it up. Plus, let's face it, sometimes her listening skills are a work in progress. (I eagerly await the day her prefrontal cortex is fully developed!)

The next day, I'm happily working on the puzzle at the kitchen table when she comes home from work and starts venting about me to my husband. I couldn't help but eavesdrop for a moment (hey, I'm only human!) I catch snippets like, "Mom is so obsessed with her stupid puzzle! She won't stop nagging me about it for days!" Oh boy, was I tempted to jump into defensive mode. I wanted to set the record straight and tell her I only reminded her twice. But then I thought, "Hold up, let it go — cue the Frozen soundtrack." But oh no, she kept on going and going. It took all my will-power to resist activating my emotional meltdown. She was completely wrong about me. Finally, when her words became a never-ending stream (as 20-somethings tend to do), I un-leashed my ultimate relationship strategy. I reminded myself that she was a human being, simply uttering sentences and words. And guess what? I got to decide what those words actually meant.

So there I sat, working on my puzzle for a solid three minutes, repeating in my mind, "Words, words, words. Look, another sentence. Sentence, sentence, sentence." It was my secret weapon against the activation monster in my head. I know I annoy my friends sometimes with this advice, but I can't help but share it. I often say, "Well, they're humans, and humans tend to communicate with words. You're the one who gets to interpret their meaning." It has actually worked wonders with my youngest when I feel the urge to offer unsolicited advice. I'll say, "Hey, I'm a human, and I'm about to say some words. If you don't like 'em, ignore 'em. If they're helpful, great! But most importantly, I'm not saying these words to upset you. So, I hope you'll find something helpful in them." Sure, she gives me that "you're a weirdo" look. But hey, after raising a bunch of kids, I'm used to that kind of reaction.

Remember, my friend, it's all about finding your own way to navigate the journey. Even when others seem determined to rain on your parade, you get to decide how their words and actions impact you. So, buckle up, embrace your quirks, and keep rocking your own unique playlist through this crazy symphony of life.

To sum up:

In conclusion, it's natural to desire a life where our ner-vous system remains untouched and undisturbed. However, such a life would likely be freaking boring as crap because it is through our interactions with other human beings that experiences unfold. Being in relationships with others means that things will inevitably happen — both positive and challenging.

To navigate these interactions with grace and maintain our inner peace, we have explored valuable tools throughout this chapter. Assuming positive intent allows us to approach others with an open heart and give them the benefit of the doubt, fostering healthier and more constructive relationships. Additionally, by becoming aware of our thought habits and patterns, we gain the power to transform negative thought patterns into more positive and empowering ones.

Additionally, intentional practices that reassure our body of safety play a vital role in restoring our equilibrium after challenging encounters. By consciously reminding ourselves that we are secure and protected, we can help our nervous system recalibrate and find its balance again. When integrated into our lives, these tools empower us to live more peacefully and consciously design our own path.

Taking responsibility for our emotional remote control is key. Rather than allowing others to push our buttons and dictate our emotional state, we become the masters of our own responses. This newfound control grants us the ability to navigate relationships and experiences with greater clarity, resilience, and self-assurance.

As you continue on your journey, may you embrace these tools and insights to live a life of deeper connection, understanding, and peace. Remember, it is within your power to shape your interactions and design a life that aligns with your values and aspirations. So take hold of your emotional remote control, and let it guide you towards a more fulfilling and harmonious existence.

CHAPTER 11
You made it

Picture this: I found myself sitting at the bustling Barcelona airport, surrounded by my trusty rolling bag and backpack. Across from me sat a friendly lady who, to my surprise, recognized me from the same cruise we had both been on. As we struck up a conversation about our shared voyage and how we ended up there, I casually mentioned that our European adventure didn't stop at the nine-day cruise with its seven exciting ports. Oh no, we had embarked on an additional ten days of exploring Paris, the scenic French countryside, and the vibrant streets of Barcelona.

Naturally, the topic of luggage came up. To my amazement, the lady confessed that she had already checked in a bag and was lugging around a massive carry-on that seemed to expand infinitely, along with a backpack. In contrast, I had managed to breeze through 19 days in Europe with just my trusty rolling bag and backpack. Her eyes widened with disbelief. How on earth did I pull it off?

I let her in on my secret. You see, while she had meticulously packed her bag with all sorts of emergency essentials to combat her fears, I had significantly tamed my own fears and lightened my load. Sure, I still had a stash of protein bars and shakes because being caught without easily accessible food is just not my style. And yes, I had a couple of extra jackets and sweaters, as my weight loss journey had made me more susceptible to feeling chilly. But overall, very few items in my bag hadn't served a purpose Gone were the days of carrying around an extra sewing kit that rarely saw the light of day. Instead, I had mastered the art of packing precisely what I needed and nothing more. It was a liberating experience, traversing three European countries with a skip in my step and minimal baggage weighing me down.

The joy of traveling light washed over me like a gentle breeze, granting me the freedom to explore and immerse myself fully in the wonders of Europe. It was a lesson in shedding unnecessary baggage, not just in the literal sense but also in life. And as I sat there, savoring the conversation with my newfound acquaintance, I couldn't help but revel in the simple joy of navigating the world with a light heart and even lighter luggage. Life can create scars that are like the stamps in a passport that create a state of existing and surviving. Traveling light gives us the flexibility to design a life worthy of living.

We're almost at the end of our time together, so I hope you'll join me in taking just a moment to recognize all the hard work you've done just to get here. Just like Luke Skywalker, you answered the hero's call and stuck with the journey –– and yourself –– all the way, which is heroic indeed! As you start to move out into the world, I have a few final reminders and invitations for you.

Many times while writing this book, I questioned whether I knew enough to write it. I am still new to the process of completing emotional cycles, even though I've been searching for many years. I had to consciously remind myself that I wanted to write it while I was still fairly new. I've experienced other people who have spent years studying this work, broadly called somatic processing, and I think they forget how difficult it was in the beginning. I've gained so much freedom that I had to share it, and I have full confidence that, just like my other book, I'll know so much more five years from now.

Pleasures I've enjoyed

As I mentioned, I'm a seek pleasure kind of girl. Some of the pleasures from the experience of clearing my emotional landmines and rehabilitating the land have been surprising.

One aspect that became apparent during my emotional healing journey was the issue of clutter. When I purchased my house two decades ago, I was enamored with the abundance of closets it offered. These storage spaces became the perfect spots to stash various items for those "just in case" moments. However, over time, I found myself not only utilizing the closets but also using every available surface, shelf, and counter as additional storage spaces. One time, during a therapy session, I found myself complaining about how my husband, Barry, wouldn't work on household projects, leaving me to tackle them alone. What I didn't confess was that I hadn't even started these projects because I was convinced he wouldn't help. In response to my whining, my therapist, usually gentle and kind, unexpectedly replied in an exasperated tone, "What can you do?" This caught me off guard, perhaps because the stern parent voice had a profound effect on me. It made me pause and reflect. So, I suggested, "Well, I can go through each room and evaluate if there's anything I don't truly love. Then, I can remove those items and have a clearer idea of what I actually need to replace."

This prompted a purge that involved removing many things hanging on my walls. I experienced significant resistance in parting with these items — they might be worth something someday, a flawed logic that came from my childhood experiences with poverty. However, a pattern emerged when I gathered all the objects on a table. I realized that they were mostly gifts from people in my life. It took weeks of contemplation to understand that I was afraid that by donating or discarding these items, I would somehow be letting go of the love these individuals had for me. It may sound silly, but these unresolved emotional attachments can create quite a mess until we confront them. Eventually, with the support and encouragement of a friend, I took pictures of

166 You made it

each item. And with newfound clarity, I was able to donate them to a non-profit thrift store. Maybe they would be worth something –– to someone else.

Embarking on this journey of emotional healing, I never anticipated the remarkable transformation it would bring, not only in releasing the clutter from my home but also in shedding excess weight. It all culminated with that profound moment of forgiveness towards my 19-year-old self, which triggered a significant shift in my relationship with my body and food. I discovered that I had been using food as a means to numb the pain, alleviate boredom, and provide comfort to myself. Similarly, alcohol had become a crutch to "take the stress off" in my life. While I cannot claim to have completed this journey entirely, as my family history predisposes me to alcoholism, I remain vigilant and aware of the potential pitfalls. This emotional exploration has heightened my self-awareness, surpassing even what I learned during my therapy sessions at 19. As I wrote this book, I decided not to drink alcohol until it was finished, originally assuming it would take no longer than a year to publish. However, editing is a different matter entirely, and I often jokingly say, editing drove me to drink. Regardless, I successfully refrained from consuming alcohol for a remarkable period of 13 months. I definitely see how abstaining for such a long time caused a dramatic shift in my identity and belief in my ability to accomplish something arduous when driven by a compelling reason.

Pain I've avoided

Besides enjoying pleasure, I also have avoided pain, much to my survival mechanism's relief. As I confronted the pain stored within the toxic waste barrels of my past, I discovered a profound truth. By avoiding the painful emotions for so long, I had unknowingly allowed them to linger, waiting for the opportune moment to resurface and wreak havoc on my well-being. It was as if these unresolved wounds had a mind of their own, ready to pounce at any given time, forcing me to relive the intense feelings all over again. I soon realized that not everything in this process was a quick fix or a one-and-done affair. Some pain demanded my patient acceptance, requiring me to hold space for it for an extended period before it finally began to release its grip on me. However, there were other wounds that, once I mustered the courage to confront and embrace them, lost their power over me entirely. The reduction of their hold brought about a newfound mental tranquility: a peaceful state in which the echoes of constant flashbacks no longer reverberated through my mind. The absence of this relentless turmoil is truly a gift, allowing me to experience the present moment fully and embrace the peace that accompanies it. By facing my pain, I have unraveled its chains and opened the door to a life of greater freedom and inner peace.

By embracing a shift in the dynamic of my inner critic, I've effectively dethroned it from the position of board chair in my mind. This powerful change has reduced the relentless pain of constantly beating myself up. Instead, I now find it easier to rest and recharge, granting myself the much-needed respite I deserve. With this newfound self-compassion, I am able to set goals for myself and navigate the inevitable twists and turns of life without spiraling into despair when things don't unfold exactly as planned. This shift in perspective has allowed me to approach setbacks with grace and resilience, recognizing that they are merely detours on the path to growth and achievement. I can now celebrate progress, both big and small, without allowing setbacks to overshadow my accomplishments. It's a liberating feeling to let go of the need for perfection and embrace the beauty of imperfection.

Efficiency I've achieved

Among the various benefits of this journey — tackling clutter, managing weight, examining reasons behind eating and drinking — one revelation stands out as particularly invaluable: the profound understanding that no one else has the power to make me feel a certain way. Sure, there are moments when people in my life say things that I find hurtful.

I'm only human, after all. However, I have developed the capacity to sit with those emotions and treat myself with gentleness. I've learned to allow the waves of emotions to rise and fall, eventually returning to a state of homeostasis. Not walking around constantly scanning the horizon for the lions that wait to attack is definitely more efficient.

Additionally, I've cultivated a greater sense of responsibility for my actions, resisting the impulses that my emotions may incite. There are times when I'm tempted to lash out in anger when I feel hurt, and I must admit that I've succumbed more often than I'd like to acknowledge. Apologizing isn't something I particularly enjoy. I prefer to avoid it altogether. However, reminding myself that I don't want to apologize later helps me exercise self-control in the present moment.

I embrace curiosity, exploring why my mind jumped to anger so quickly. In most cases, it boils down to protection, a survival mechanism that remains finely attuned within me. I've even learned to share my concern out loud by saying, "I don't know why this is upsetting me so much." Sometimes I don't uncover the root cause; I simply allow the sensations to exist and focus on deep breathing as a means of navigating through them.

Hero's Journey: be the hero, and embrace your fear

As I mentioned earlier, I have a strong fascination with Joseph Campbell's concept of the hero's journey. I completely understand the desire to be the hero in your own story, and I hope that you can relate to this as well! Hopefully, we can all be the Luke Skywalker of our own story, and I hope you are also sometimes Leia, the strong ally, and in other situations still, I hope you are the all-wise Yoda or the bold Han Solo.

The purpose of this book is to guide you on your own hero's journey. Let me briefly recap the progress we've made together.

It all begins with the hero receiving a call to adventure, for which you might have been picking up this book. The journey is intentionally designed to push you out of your comfort zone. However, just like we discussed the "window of tolerance," you have the capacity to expand your comfort zone by taking risks. As you read the initial chapters, you may have discovered how your brain works and learned about the fight/flight/freeze response, which is hardwired in us for survival. Exploring the concept of making sense of things probably wasn't too terrifying, either.

Next, the hero often refuses the call. During the chapters on beliefs and emotions, you might have felt hesitant to fully embrace my perspective on these topics. Perhaps you had never really considered the distinction between feelings and emotions before, or maybe it was challenging for you to openly admit that you struggle with feeling good enough.

But fear not! Every hero encounters a mentor along their journey, and I hope you recognize that I'm here to provide you with encouragement and support rather than judgment. As you read about how I simplify the understanding of feeling sensations, you may have felt a bit less apprehensive and more receptive to new ideas.

With your mentor's guidance and assistance, you faced challenges, gathered valuable tools and allies, and underwent a transformative process. By developing techniques to calm your nervous system's response, adopting new empowering beliefs, and becoming a better friend to yourself and others, you were able to overcome your personal fears and insecurities. These were the dragons that once made you believe you were perpetually flawed or trapped.

Now, you stand victorious, and it's time to celebrate your accomplishments and share the newfound freedom you've attained with others.

In a similar vein to how the inner critic can take on a new role in your life, I want to discuss the role of fear. Fear itself is neither inherently good nor bad. It simply represents your body's response to danger. To help illustrate this, I've come to think of fear as Chewbacca. Just like Chewie fear can be a great ally. You can't fully understand it unless you speak its language, and sometimes it might lead you to react defensively, much like Chewbacca's tendency to throw punches at friends — but always with the intention of protecting Han Solo.

Your fear is similar in nature. It serves as an indicator, perhaps suggesting that you need to slow down, consider a backup plan, or express gratitude to your fear for attempting to keep you safe. Instead of trying to eliminate or "slay" your fear, I encourage you to establish a friendship with it. Make it an ally in your journey, just like Han Solo did with Chewbacca.

Share recommendations

Have you ever noticed that when you're traveling somewhere new, you research like crazy? You read reviews or may post on social media asking for insider tips. Think about when a friend is going to visit somewhere you've been. Isn't it fun to share restaurants you've visited, excursions you took, and things you learned about that place? It's like reliving your vacation again. You remember the fun and the challenges and have the feelings again. When we get back from trips, we love to share the details of what happened, share the photos on social media, and relive the experience as much as possible.

As you journey through life, I hope you'll see the path you've taken as we do vacations. I hope you'll share your stories, including the ones that weren't pleasant, not in a complaining way, but in a way to share the learning you experienced. You made mistakes along the way. Why would you stand next to an open manhole and not alert people of the potential danger so they could walk around the manhole and avoid falling in?

Social media has programmed us to share a glossy, happy life. Or to be overly dramatic when faced with a minor setback. Let's settle that pendulum in the middle. Not every pain is meant to be shared on social media, but can you make a point to share some of the real? I've found that when you share the pain you have and what you are learning from the situation, it comes from a place of authenticity, not complaining. I check myself first. Am I sharing something to get sympathy for how hard my life is? If so, I might not be in the right frame of mind to share. If I'm sharing to provide a way marker for others so they avoid the manhole, I'm typically in a better place to tell the story.

My therapist said that most of us aren't willing to tell our story during the messy middle. Our brains want the safety of knowing how the story ends. It takes a lot of courage to tell the story, not knowing if the hero is victorious yet. Tell your story anyway.

It's time to get moving!

You've done so much work to get here and gone on such a journey throughout this book. But the journey's not over -- and now it's time to make a shift.

Throughout life's epic journey, you will need many forms of transportation. Sometimes you'll need the slow, stop-and-go of public transportation. This will be when you think you have an idea of how to get to your goal, but you may not have all the resources you need. You use crowdsourced resources like free information on the internet to learn what you need to learn. At some points in your journey, you will have a definite idea of where you want to go, but it will take a long road trip to get there. This trip will allow you to stop along the way to enjoy the scenery and pick up skills you didn't have or needed to practice. Parts of your life journey may be like traveling in a sailboat, where you depend on the wind to give you the speed you need. When I was 29, God seemed to whisper to me that he designed me to stand at the helm, but He would be the wind in my sails. Still, other parts of your life will be like traveling by plane.

You may have to wait in line and clear some emotional blocks, but you'll get to your destination faster. This may be like hiring a therapist or coach -- the process may involve discomfort -- but you'll get to start enjoying your life faster.

172 You made it

When we travel, we rely on others along the way. So I hope you pay it forward by sharing what you've learned with fellow travelers and giving tips on places you've visited.

My earnest hope is that you take the journey while traveling light. Don't sit on the sidelines, allowing your past mistakes, hurts, and fears to hold you back. I hope when you imagine your 90th birthday, you imagine I will be there, cheering you on -- encouraging you to be brave, make friends with your fear, and never stop evolving.

If you do, it will be epic.

Acknowledgments

I've put off writing this section because of the fear of forgetting someone. But alas, here we go.

If you've been within 6 feet of me from 2021-2023, you've probably heard about my book and/or gotten into a conversation that helped me articulate something I was noodling. Thank you.

Dick Suits – posthumously – you were with me for so much of the journey of this book. Your joy for life, your belief in me, and your love for your family will continue to ripple across generations.

Rachel Allen – you did what I wasn't sure could be done, helped me create a book I love. I will be forever grateful for your patience, diligence, and partnership in bringing this book to fruition. I hope you are as happy with the outcome as I am.

The Belford Group team – Shannon, Erica, Elizabeth, Hilary, and Kat – from reading early manuscripts, final proofing, and attention to detail on the cover and layout of the manuscript to updating the website and editing the podcast – thank you for everything. Also for taking great care of our clients no matter where in the world I am.

CCP Life Coach cohort – Emma, Sylvia, Neha, Miho, Becky, and Srihari – thank you for your weekly support for nearly two years as well as for being willing to try out my program which made it so much better.

Molly – my fellow author buddy – I'm so grateful for our regular catch-ups, your encouragement of my journey, and so many referrals. It's lovely to have a fellow traveler who's also such good friends with Jesus.

Fritz and LeaLea – so many hours spent on your couch safely exploring the latest thing I'm trying to figure out. Thank you for laughter, unconditional love & acceptance, and for challenging my thoughts in a way that makes them better and stronger. I adore that miles or months don't diminish the relationship.

Marcia – the Lord knew what I needed and allowed us to cross paths. Thank you for letting me sit on the deck especially in the early days of writing to ponder what I was learning. So much gratitude for your willingness to read very early rough drafts of this book and to encourage the diamond in the rough you saw. Your support and belief were hugely helpful.

Lexi – thanks for sticking with your journey of healing so we can continue to build a fun relationship which gives me so much hope for restoration in this world. You provide a beautiful example of a committed friend and I love watching you become more of who you were born to be every day.

Josh – when you agreed to be my podcast host (or did I finally agree to be your co-host) it meant so much and you bring joy to me with your practical approach to the work I do. Your unwillingness to read my first book since it was just how you were raised is a glowing compliment, even if you didn't intend it. I look forward to watching you and Abby grow together.

Sami – who knew it was possible to give birth to one of your very best friends? Your belief in me and this work is awe-inspiring. Your attention to detail, willingness to wade into hard conversations, and playfulness are a gift to me as well as the business we are building together.

Barry – so many chapters of our life looked like they were heading for the end of marriage. Instead, we've continued to put together a combination of tenacity, growth, and God's rich blessings. According to Ryan, our marriage counselor, our commitment to a great sex life has helped also. Thank you for believing in me and being the best travel buddy ever, including continuing to Travel Light.